# The Ultimate Guide to
# WEIGHT TRAINING for FIELD HOCKEY

Prior to beginning any exercise program, you must consult with your physician. You must also consult your physician before increasing the intensity of your training.

Any application of the recommended material in this book is at the sole risk of the reader, and at the reader's discretion. Responsibility of any injuries or other negative effects resulting from the application of any of the information provided within this book is expressly disclaimed.

Published by Price World Enterprises
5815 Landerbrook Drive
P.O. Box 24434
Cleveland, OH 44124

Book design and layout by Alexandru Dan Georgescu
Book design by Jeff Ross
Cover design by Alexandru Dan Georgescu
Interior photographs by Marc Gollub
Editing by Barb Greenberg
Editing and proofreading by Maryanne Haselow-Dulin
Printing by Express Media

First edition: June 2003
ISBN: 1-932549-09-9

Printed in the United States of America

10  9  8  7  6  5  4  3  2  1

Special thanks to:
Dr. Marc B. Price CPFT for your expert insight and helpful contributions
Zack, David, and Gail Price for your support and encouragement to make this book possible.

# The Ultimate Guide to
# WEIGHT
# TRAINING
## for FIELD
# HOCKEY

**sports**workout.com

# CONTENTS

# Part I
# YEAR-ROUND PROGRAM

## Introduction

By opening *The Ultimate Guide to Weight Training for Field Hockey*, you have taken your first step towards achieving your athletic potential. This book is loaded with the most up-to-date sports weight training information and features a year-round field hockey-specific weight-training program. Upon completion of the text, you will know how to properly, safely, and effectively perform over 80 exercises and you will be ready to begin your training.

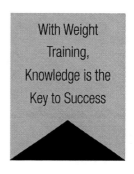

With Weight Training, Knowledge is the Key to Success

The true importance of this book lies in the field hockey-specific program in the front of the book. It was created for one reason and one reason only; to improve your field hockey potential. It does this by increasing your strength, explosion, power, endurance, and flexibility in the parts of your body that are most important for field hockey. The program was designed to supply you with the advantage you will need to outperform your opponents. By following the program, you will build your muscles with strength and endurance as well as explosion, power, and agility. When called upon, you will be physically prepared and mentally ready to compete at the highest of your potential.

Although the sport of field hockey is primarily a sport focusing on leg strength and endurance, there are certain upper-body muscle groups that should not be ignored in order to achieve your maximum potential. *The Ultimate Guide to Weight Training for Field Hockey* does not overlook the importance of these muscle groups and has you training your entire body in order to maximize your potential.

This book does not teach you how to perform specific movements. It does not show you the best strategies to maneuver past your opponent, nor does it give you any tips to improve your specific skills. This book does, however, provide you with the best methods, program, and strategies available to physically improve your body and maximize your field hockey potential!

# Off-Season Training

The off-season is the time in any sport to build up your muscles, become stronger, and more powerful. The off-season program consists of four different four-week routines cycled together to build both absolute strength and explosive power. The first and third routines are designed for you to put on size and strength while the second and fourth programs are designed for power and explosion.

> After following the first two 4-week off-season programs, be sure to take one week away from the gym to let your muscles rest and grow stronger before beginning your final two 4-week programs.

Variation is one of the keys to a great workout program. The most important reason to vary your routines is so you can continue making progress and gains. Your body will eventually adapt to any routine it's on, so it is very important to change routines once your gains have stopped and your strength has peaked. Four weeks is the most effective time period to follow any one routine. For more information on the importance of variation to weight training look in *The Ultimate Guide to Weight Training for Sports.*

It cannot be stressed enough that during the off-season, you must supplement your weight-training activities with some sort of sport-specific activities to keep your body in proper shape. You must continue to practice your skills throughout the off-season to help keep your body loose and ready to for the next season.

## Strength Training

The stronger the vital areas of your body are, the better off you will be. Although some muscles are more important than others, every muscle in your body needs to be well trained. Five important aspects to strength training that the book provides:

**Compound exercises:** Each program contains many compound exercises, that is, an exercise (such as squats, bench presses, and lat pull downs) that trains two or more muscle groups. Most exercise and strength-training experts agree that compound exercises are the most efficient exercises for building strength and size.

**Great form:** For the best results, use great form while training. Take at least two seconds on the eccentric (negative) phase of the lift and at least one second on the concentric (positive) phase of the lift. This slow, rhythmic movement builds your muscles up bigger and stronger than any other type of lifting.

**Pyramid Method:** Several exercises in the strength-building routines are structured in a pyramid method of sets and reps, which is another strength-building tactic designed to maximize your efforts in the gym. When using the pyramid method, you decrease the reps and increase the load with every set.

1

333

55555

**Heavy weights, low reps:** Building strength effectively requires lifting heavy weights between 1 and 8 repetitions for each set. Working to failure with fewer reps and heavier weights is the most effective way to put on strength and size quickly. To achieve the fastest and most effective results, train your muscles with the heaviest weights possible while still using good form. In most cases, people are able to lift heavier weights with barbells than dumbbells, which is why barbell exercises dominate strength programs. For optimal results, lift weights that are at least 85% of your one rep max.

You can safely estimate your one rep max for any exercise using a one rep max calculator at www.sportsworkout.com.

**Extended rest time:** By lifting such heavy weights, your muscles fatigue very quickly and need more rest time between sets than the other types of training. Generally two to five minutes between sets is ample time to rest. This rest time brings your heart rate back down closer to its resting rate so you are fully ready to complete another strenuous set with heavy weights.

# Explosive-Power Training

The second and fourth routines of the cycle are designed to build speed and explosive power. Four important aspects to explosive power training are:

**Medium weights, medium reps:** Training for power is quite different than training for strength. For strength training, the idea is to lift heavy weights a low number of times. Contrastingly, decreasing the weight-load and lifting between eight and fifteen repetitions is the best way to successfully train for power and explosion.

**Speed and intensity:** With power training, the goal is to increase the speed while lifting. Before increasing the load, you want to increase the speed at which you are performing the concentric part, or positive phase of the lift. If the load begins to feel extremely light, then follow the steps listed in The Ultimate Guide to Weight Training for Sports for increasing the resistance.

There are certain exercises, however, that should never be performed with speed and intensity due to the possibility of injury, or because fast movements are not as effective as slow ones. Exercises listed in our programs that should never be lifted with speed and intensity are:

1. Lower back exercises
2. Rotator cuff exercises
3. Mid-section exercises

**Great Form:** Similar to strength training, the lowering of the weight should be smooth and slow for at least two seconds. The difference comes on the concentric part of the lift. For power training you want to raise the weights as fast and explosively as possible. This works your fast-twitch muscle fibers with the goal of increasing the speed that you can contract and move your muscles. While following power-building routines, you are required to perform the concentric part of every rep in every set with intensity and speed. On a very important note, however, you must be sure to not sacrifice form for speed. Always make sure you perform the lift the proper way as instructed.

**Power exercises:** Certain exercises are most beneficial and most effectively performed with speed and intensity. Olympic lifts such as push presses and power cleans, as well as body weight exercises like dips, and pull-ups are such examples because they can be performed extremely fast with enormous amounts of intensity.

You will notice that a small number of low rep exercises for strength training are included to compliment the explosive power training. It is necessary that any explosive power weight-training program include at least some strength building aspects in order to maintain the strength you have acquired during the strength-training cycle. This ensures that upon completion of the first explosive power training routine, you will be able to start back up on the second strength-building program without losing any strength.

Remember to: -Train your abs prior to each training session
-Stretch your muscles directly after each training session

### Field Hockey Off-Season Program
Strength and Power Cycle

### Weeks 1-4 Strength Training

Days1 & 3

| muscle group | exercise | sets | reps |
|---|---|---|---|
| chest | dumbbell bench press | 5 | 8,6,4,2,1 |
| back | one-arm dumbbell rows | 4 | 8,8,8,8 |
| chest | incline dumbbell bench press | 5 | 8,6,4,2,1 |
| shoulders | dumbbell military press | 5 | 10,8,6,4,2 |
| legs | leg curls | 5 | 8,6,4,2,1 |
| legs | seated calf raises | 4 | 20,20,20,20 |
| forearms | behind back wrist curls | 4 | 8,8,8,8 |

Days2 & 4

| muscle group | exercise | sets | reps |
|---|---|---|---|
| legs | leg press | 5 | 10,8,6,4,2 |
| legs | lunges | 5 | 10,8,6,4,2 |
| triceps | triceps kickbacks | 4 | 12,10,8,6 |
| triceps | skull crushers | 5 | 12,10,8,6,2 |
| bi's/forearms | hammer curls | 4 | 12,10,8,6 |
| triceps | dumbbell triceps curls | 4 | 12,10,8,6 |
| forearms | wrist curls | 4 | 8,8,8,8 |

## Weeks 5-8 Power Training

Days1 & 3

| muscle group | exercise | sets | reps |
|---|---|---|---|
| chest | dumbbell bench press | 3 | 10,10,10 |
| back | wide-grip pull-ups | 2 | failure |
| shoulders | push press | 3 | 12,12,12 |
| legs | leg curls | 3 | 12,12,12 |
| legs | calf raises | 3 | 20,20,20 |
| chest/shoulders | dips | 2 | failure |

Days2 & 4

| muscle group | exercise | sets | reps |
|---|---|---|---|
| legs | box steps | 3 | 12,12,12 |
| legs | power cleans | 3 | 12,12,12 |
| triceps | bench dips | 2 | failure |
| triceps | triceps curls | 4 | 12,12,12,12 |
| bi's/forearms | hammer curls | 3 | 12,12,12 |
| triceps | skull crushers | 4 | 12,12,12,12 |

## Weeks 9-12 Strength Training

Days1 & 3

| muscle group | exercise | sets | reps |
|---|---|---|---|
| chest | dumbbell bench press | 5 | 8,6,4,2,1 |
| back | close-grip lat pull downs | 4 | 8,8,8,8 |
| shoulders | dumbbell military press | 5 | 8,6,4,2,1 |
| legs | leg curls | 5 | 10,8,6,4,2 |
| legs/low back | good mornings | 4 | 15,15,15,15 |
| chest | incline dumbbell bench | 5 | 8,6,4,2,1 |

Days2 & 4

| muscle group | exercise | sets | reps |
|---|---|---|---|
| legs | squats | 5 | 10,8,6,4,2 |
| legs | dead lift | 5 | 10,8,6,4,2 |
| biceps | preacher curls | 4 | 12,10,8,6 |
| triceps | triceps push downs | 4 | 12,10,8,6 |
| bi's/forearms | reverse curls | 4 | 12,10,8,6 |
| triceps | triceps kickbacks | 4 | 12,10,8,6 |
| bi's/forearms | hammer curls | 4 | 8,8,6,6 |

### Weeks 13-16 Power Training

Days1 & 3

| muscle group | exercise | sets | reps |
|---|---|---|---|
| chest | dumbbell bench press | 3 | 12,12,12 |
| back | close-grip pull-ups | 3 | failure |
| shoulders | push press | 3 | 12,12,12 |
| legs | leg curls | 3 | 15,15,15 |
| legs | calf raises | 3 | 20,20,20 |
| chest/shoulders | dips | 3 | failure |

Days2 & 4

| muscle group | exercise | sets | reps |
|---|---|---|---|
| legs | power cleans | 3 | 10,10,10 |
| legs | jump squats | 3 | 12,12,12 |
| biceps | concentration curls | 4 | 15,15,15,15 |
| triceps | dumbbell triceps curls | 4 | 15,15,15,15 |
| triceps | dips | 3 | failure |
| bi's/forearms | Reverse curls | 3 | 12,12,12 |

# In-Season Training

## Maintenance Training

While in season, the preferred method of training is for maintenance. The goal of in-season weight training is to maintain the gains you have acquired during the off-season, while being careful not to over train and become stale. When you become stale, your abilities and performance as an athlete decrease drastically. Lifting weights more than twice a week and practicing on a daily basis is more than enough to over train many people.

In order to maintain the endurance and explosion added in the off-season, in-season maintenance training calls for working out your major sport-specific muscle groups two days a week. This type of training is twice a week because it is the least number of days required to lift while still maintaining your gains. Training your muscles only once a week can cause them to lose the gains that they have acquired. The in-season routine includes maintenance exercises for endurance, strength, and explosive power elements so that nothing is lost during the season. If you wish, you can perform the in-season routine using a *circuit training* format. For more information on circuit training, see the *Training Techniques* section.

# Field Hockey In-Season Program

### Maintenance Training

### Train two days per week

**Odd Weeks**

Days 1 & 2

| muscle group | exercise | sets | reps |
|---|---|---|---|
| chest | dumbbell bench press | 3 | 10,10,10 |
| back | one-arm dumbbell rows | 3 | 10,10,10 |
| shoulders | dumbbell military press | 3 | 10,10,10 |
| biceps/forearms | hammer curls | 3 | 10,10,10 |
| legs | squats | 3 | 10,10,10 |
| legs | standing calf raises | 2 | 20,20 |

**Even Weeks**

Days 1 & 2

| muscle group | exercise | sets | reps |
|---|---|---|---|
| chest | flyes | 3 | 10,10,10 |
| back | seated cable rows | 3 | 10,10,10 |
| shoulders | upright rows | 3 | 10,10,10 |
| biceps/forearms | hammer curls | 3 | 10,10,10 |
| legs | leg press | 3 | 10,10,10 |
| legs | leg curls | 2 | 10,10,10 |

## Warming Up

Warming up is an essential part of a weight-training routine. *A warm-up activity can be any type of low-level activity as long as it loosens up your body, gets your blood flowing, and prepares your body for the workout.* Warming up is absolutely necessary if you plan to lift heavy weights. To walk into the gym and attempt to *max out* (lift the maximum amount of weight you can handle) without first warming up can cause injury because your body is not ready for the physical stress of a weight-training routine. In general, there are two major types of warming up, which are listed below.

A **full body warm-up** is anything that increases your blood flow and literally warms you up. Examples of full-body warm-up activities include low-intensity activities such as jogging or riding the bike for five to ten minutes prior to lifting weights. Other examples include about five to ten minutes of an abdominal routine, swimming a few laps, or even some full-body stretching.

An **exercise-specific warm-up** is properly executed by performing a light-weight *set* (group of repetitions) of an exercise before going into your prescribed routine for that same exercise with heavier weights. Ten repetitions are usually enough for a warm-up set. Basing your exercise-specific warm-up set on half of your *one-rep max* is the best technique. Your one-rep max is the maximum weight you can lift one time. Performing an exercise-specific warm-up increases your blood flow to the *active muscles*, that is, the muscles you are using.

Warm-up sets should be performed with weights that are about half of your one-rep max. To determine your one rep max, log on to **www.sportsworkout.com** and use the one-rep max calculator.

**Benefits of Warming Up** One major benefit of warming up is that it helps reduce the likelihood of pulls, tears, and other injuries, which can be painful and hamper your future training. Another major benefit of warming up is that it loosens your muscles and allows you to lift heavier weights. Heavier weights, in turn, put more resistance on your muscles, which forces you work to harder and gives you a better workout.

# Cooling Down

Cooling-down activities come directly after your weight-training session. While cooling down, the goal is, again, to loosen up your muscles. In this book, cool-down activities are synonymous with stretching exercises. Cooling-down activities are important because they can prevent soreness in the days following a weight-training session. They also increase your range of motion, helping you become more flexible, which can prevent injuries both in the weight room and in athletics. Because flexibility and range of motion are so important for all sports, stretching is a vital part of a complete workout program and should never be ignored.

There are numerous benefits to stretching and it is most effective during or after your workout. Stretching increases your range of motion and ***stretching can be effective in injury reduction.*** Proper stretching *may* also be effective in reducing soreness from weight training by helping to remove the anaerobic waste product—lactate—from your muscles.

Range of motion is essential for all sports and physical activities, and stretching is the way to increase it. It is a myth that weight training automatically makes you stiff and decreases your flexibility. Training ***antagonistic***, or opposite, muscle groups in the same session actually stretches your muscles and helps increase your range of motion. An example of an antagonistic muscle group is the biceps and triceps. As the biceps contract, the triceps extend, which gives them a nice, full stretch.

# Abs

Having a tight stomach, strong lower back, and incredible six-pack is important for both personal and athletic reasons. The exercises provided in this book will have you training properly and building picture-perfect abs. Lower back and oblique exercises are also incorporated with the abs routine so that your entire torso becomes stronger. Having strong abdominals is essential for high sports performance. With tight abs and a strong lower back, you will be able to run faster and become more explosive. You will also be able to make quicker movements with your torso, which leads to jumping higher and making sharper turns and cuts. Your midsection connects your upper body to your lower body, and it allows you to apply the strength and power collectively in both areas. A stronger midsection will increase your athletic capabilities.

By nature, the muscles in your midsection are different from the other muscles in your body and need to be trained differently in order to achieve maximum results. To train your abs properly, you need the following:

**1. Slow movements:** Abs are made up mostly of slow-twitch muscle fibers, which requires them to be trained with slow movements for optimal results. More information on slow- and fast-twitch fibers can be found in *The Ultimate Guide to Weight Training for Sports.*

**2. Quantity and consistency:** Abdominals need to be trained for muscular endurance, not muscular strength, which requires many, many repetitions that can be performed daily.

**3. Variety:** Your midsection consists of different areas, each of which requires different exercises. To train each area, you need to perform a variety of exercises. Variety with any exercise is an essential part of muscle building and athletic training. Variety allows you to build and tone every part of the muscle you are training.

To keep things simple, this book refers to the areas of the abdomen as the:

- **Upper Abs**
- **Lower Abs**
- **Obliques**

## Preferred Order of Training

Lower abs and oblique exercises are *compound exercises,* that is, they train more than one muscle group at a time. These exercises also train your upper abs. Upper abs exercises, on the other hand, strictly isolate your upper abs. In order to avoid fatigue in the upper abs, which are being worked in every type of abdominal exercise, and could prevent proper lower abs and obliques training, you should train the lower abs first, then the obliques, and lastly the upper abs.

The preferred order of training your abdominals is as follows:
- **Lower Abs**
- **Obliques**
- **Upper Abs**

**Note**: You can train your lower back before or after performing your abdominal exercises, depending on your personal preference.

Training your midsection for at least five minutes prior to lifting is a great way to warm up because you are both warming yourself up by increasing your blood flow, and you are also building and toning your entire midsection. This can be thought of this as killing two birds with one stone. Perform each exercise slowly and smoothly for one full minute without rest. Rest for 30 seconds between exercises.

Listed below are descriptions and pictures demonstrating exactly how to perform each of the recommended midsection exercises. Do not be overwhelmed by the vast number of recommended exercises. You only need to pick four or five of them for each warm-up routine. As your midsection becomes stronger, you should increase the number of exercises you perform so that you continue progressing in strength. Vary your routine constantly by choosing four or five exercises to warm up with one day and a completely new set of four or five exercises the next day.

# Abs Exercises

**Definition:** *Prime movers* are the muscles being directly trained in the exercise.

## Standard Sit-ups

Prime Movers: Upper abs
Starting Position: Lie flat on your back with your knees bent and the soles of your feet flat on the floor. Elevate your tailbone about one inch above the floor. Place your hands on your ears.

Use your abs to lift the upper half of your body as high as you can, hold the position for a second or two, then slowly return to your starting position.

*Tip: By keeping your tailbone elevated, you are working your lower abs, which is a target area for many people.*

## Standard Crunches

Prime Movers: Upper abs
Starting Position: Lie flat on your back with your feet and knees elevated so that your shins are parallel with the floor. Elevate your tailbone about one inch above the floor. Place your hands on your ears.

Use your abs to lift the upper half of your body. Once you've lifted your shoulders about thirty degrees off the floor, hold the position for a second or two, then slowly return to the starting position and repeat.

## Oblique Crunches

Prime Movers: Obliques
Starting Position: Lie on your left side with your legs slightly bent, knees elevated about an inch or two above the floor, and your hands on your ears. Twist your torso to the right and do your best to keep your upper back and shoulders parallel with the floor.

Use your obliques and upper abs to lift your upper body as high as you can and hold for a second or two. Return slowly to the starting position, and repeat. Then perform this exercise lying on your right side.

## Tailbone Lifts

Prime Movers: Lower abs

**Starting Position:** Lie flat on your back with your feet and knees elevated so that your shins are parallel with the floor and place your hands on your ears.

With your stomach flexed, use your lower abs to raise your tailbone an inch or two off the floor. Hold that position for a second or two before lowering your tailbone back to the floor. Be sure to keep your upper body in the same position throughout the entire range of motion.

## Elbow to Knee Sit-ups

Prime Movers: Entire torso

**Starting Position:** Lie flat on your back with  your knees bent and the soles of your feet flat the floor. Place your hands on your ears.

Use your abs to raise your upper body forward while lifting your left foot off the floor so that your

knee comes towards your head. Touch your knee to its opposite elbow. Hold that position for a second or two with your abs flexed. Slowly lower yourself back to the starting position and repeat the same movements with your right knee and left elbow.

## Bicycles

Prime Movers: Entire torso

**Starting Position:** Lie flat on your back with your knees bent, legs extended, feet elevated a few inches above the floor, and your hands on your ears.

Use your abs to raise your upper body forward. At the same time, begin to slowly pump your legs one by one as if you were riding a bicycle. As your knee comes towards to your head, touch your raised knee to its opposite elbow. Hold that position for a second or two with your abs flexed. Go back to the starting point and repeat the same movements with your other knee and elbow.

## Side Bends

Prime Movers: Obliques

**Starting Position:** Standing upright, hold a dumbbell in your left hand and place your right hand on your head.

Lean your upper body a few inches to the left and use your obliques on the right side of your body to return to the starting position.

## Good Mornings

Prime Movers: Lower back

**Starting Position**: Stand upright with your feet close together. Rest a barbell behind your neck on your traps. Keep your head tilted back and your back completely straight.

Slowly bend at the waist until you form a ninety-degree angle with your lower body. Slowly return to the starting position and repeat.

## Hyperextensions

Prime Movers: Lower back

**Starting Position:** Lie face down on a hyperextension bench. Bend at the waist with your upper body hanging straight down and your hands placed behind your neck. Tilt your head back and keep your back straight.

Slowly raise your upper body until it is parallel with the floor and level with your lower body. Slowly return to the starting position and repeat.

*Tip for hyperextensions and the preceding exercise, good mornings: Do not arch your back at any point because it can result in a painful injury*

## Reach Throughs

Prime Movers: Upper and lower abs

**Starting Position:** Lie flat on your back with your legs extended, slightly spread apart, and elevated a few

inches above the floor. Extend both your arms behind
your head.

Use your abs to lift the upper half of your
body up and bring your knees upward so
that your shins are parallel with the floor.
Simultaneously extend your arms directly in
front of you, between your legs. Hold the
position for a second or two, slowly return to
the starting position, and repeat.

## Leg Raises

Prime Movers: Lower abs

**Starting Position**: Lie on the floor with your legs extended
and your shoulders and head tilted forward off the floor,
putting stress on your upper abs. Place your hands
underneath your tailbone to keep it slightly elevated
above the floor. Keep your upper body stationary, hands
underneath your tailbone, and legs locked throughout the
entire range of motion.

Raise your legs off the floor until they form a
ninety-degree angle with the floor, allowing
your tailbone and lower back to come off the
floor in the process. Slowly lower your legs back to the starting position and repeat.

*Tip: To get your legs that high may require a thrust from your abs, which in this case is okay.*

## Intercostal Pull Overs

Prime Movers: Intercostals

**Starting Position**: Lie on a bench
with a barbell resting on your
chest and your head slightly off
the bench. Hold the bar with an
overhand grip.

Slowly lift and lower
the bar just over and behind your head until you feel a nice stretch in your chest. At this point raise the
bar back over your head to the starting position.

*Tip: If having your head partially off of the bench feels awkward and difficult, then perform this
exercise with your head resting on the bench.*

# Stretching

Stretching is an absolutely crucial part to weight training for sports. It loosens you up, increases your range of motion, and may reduce the chance of injury and soreness in the days following a workout or athletic competition. Stretching is directly related to flexibility. This section goes into depth on how to properly stretch your muscles during or after a workout.

Everyone knows that stretching increases flexibility, but not everyone knows that lack of stretching decreases flexibility.

The recommended time for holding each stretch is ten seconds, resting thirty seconds between stretches. While holding a stretch, do not bounce; the stretch is less effective and can cause painful injuries. For every exercise, stretch as far as you can until you feel slight discomfort in the targeted areas. Go no farther once you reach that point. Hold that position for ten seconds as steadily as you can. Proper breathing and technique are extremely important. Do not hold your breath at any time during the stretch. The recommended stretching exercises and their descriptions and pictures are listed below.

## Stretching Exercises

### Hamstrings, Legs Crossed

Muscles stretched: Hamstrings.

**Starting position**: Stand upright and cross your left foot over your right, keeping your legs straight. Bending at the waist, reach as far down as you can, and hold. Repeat with other leg.

## Hamstrings, Legs Spread

Muscles stretched: Hamstrings, groin.

**Starting Position:** Stand upright and spread your legs slightly wider than shoulder width, keeping them straight.

Bending at the waist, reach as far down as you can to the outside leg and hold. Repeat to the other leg, then reach straight down. Rest between each stretch.

## Hurdler Stretch

Muscles stretched: Hamstrings, quadriceps.

**Starting Position:** Sit on the floor with your right leg extended in front of you and your left leg bent at the knee and pointing behind you.

Bend at the waist and reach as far forward as you can to your right leg and hold.

Repeat with left leg extended.

## Sit and Reach

Muscles stretched: Hamstrings, lower back.

**Starting Position:** Sit on the floor with both legs extended in front of you.

Reach forward as far as you can towards your feet, and hold.

## Standing Quad Stretch

Muscles stretched: Quadriceps.

**Starting Position:** Stand upright on your left leg.

Grab your right ankle and pull it back as far as you can towards your buttocks and hold.

Repeat with other leg.

## Neck Rolls

Muscles stretched:  Neck.

> **Starting Position:** Stand upright with your hands on your hips.
>
> Slowly roll your head clockwise in a circular motion using your full range of motion for ten rotations. Repeat going counterclockwise.

## Across Body Arm Pulls

Muscles stretched:  Shoulders, upper back.

> **Starting Position:** Stand or sit upright with your back straight. Reach across your body with your left arm.  Use your right hand to lightly pull and stretch the left arm as far and as close to your body as you can and hold. Repeat with other arm.

## Overhead Arm Pulls

Muscles stretched:  Triceps, shoulders, upper back.

> **Starting Position:** Stand or sit upright with your back straight.
> Reach up and behind your neck with your left arm.  Use your right hand to lightly pull and stretch your left arm as far as you can and hold. Repeat with other arm.

## Butterflies

Muscles stretched:  Groin, hips.

> **Starting Position**: Sit upright with your back straight and legs tucked in.

> Touch the soles of your shoes together and hold your toes with your hands.  Pull your feet in as close as you can to your body.
>
> With your elbows, lightly push your knees towards the floor as far as you can and hold.

### Seated Back Twists

Muscles stretched: Lower back, trunk, thighs, and hips.

      **Starting Position:** Sit upright with your back straight and left leg extended. Bend and cross your right leg over your left. Place your left forearm on the outside of your right leg, your right hand resting palm down on the floor next to you for balance. Twist your body to the right as far as you can and hold. Repeat to the other side.

### Lying Knee Grabs

Muscles stretched: Glutes, hips.

      **Starting Position:** Lying flat on your back with your left knee bent and right leg extended, clasp your hands over the upper shin of your left knee.

      Gently pull your left leg towards your chest until you feel the stretch and hold.

      Repeat with other leg.

### Standing Calves Stretch

Muscles stretched: Calves.

      **Starting Position:** Stand leaning forward with your arms in front of you and your hands pushing against a wall. Place your left leg in front of the right.

      Bend your left knee while keeping your right heel flat on the floor. Lean as far forward as you can while still keeping your back heel on the floor and hold.

      Repeat with other leg.

      *Tip: This exercise also can be performed with both feet back.*

# Proper Form

## Short- vs. Long-Term Results

In order to make the greatest gains in the least amount of time, you must perform each exercise properly. Lifting weights with bad form is very dangerous and can result in injury. Also, performing an exercise improperly is a waste of time in the gym. Though you may be able to lift heavier weights with improper form, your long-term results would suffer because you would not get as good a workout. You are better off working out for thirty minutes per day with excellent form and technique than lifting for three hours per day with improper form.

There are two movements to lifting a weight: the eccentric (negative) phase and the concentric (positive) phase.

**The eccentric (negative) phase of the lift** is the slow lowering of the weight. During this phase, your muscle is getting longer while still contracting. For example, in the bench press the eccentric phase occurs when you slowly lower the bar to your chest, lengthening your pectorals and triceps. Regardless of your purpose, the eccentric phase of the lift should always be slow and smooth, lasting at least two seconds. Always inhale while performing the eccentric phase of the lift.

For the best results, the eccentric phase of every lift should last for at least two seconds.

**The concentric (positive) phase of the lift** is the exertion phase, or actual lifting of the weight. During this phase, the muscle shortens and the muscle cells contract. For example, in the bench press the concentric phase occurs when you lift the bar up from your chest so that your pectorals and triceps contract. The concentric phase of every lift should last at least one second unless you are training for power and explosion, where you lift the weight concentrically as fast as you can. Always exhale while performing the concentric phase of the lift.

# Proper Breathing

**DO NOT HOLD YOUR BREATH while lifting!** Holding your breath can build up pressure in your body. Although extremely rare, if the pressure becomes extraordinarily intense, it can cut off blood circulation to your heart and brain. To avoid problems, just remember to breathe. Remember, you will get the most out of your lifting by inhaling on the eccentric part of the lift and exhaling while performing the concentric part of the lift.

INHALE on the **eccentric** part of every lift,
and **EXHALE** on the **concentric** part of every lift.

**Important note:** If you have the determination to get to the gym for a set amount of time, then train with proper form and intensity so that you spend your time efficiently. Many people come home from the gym and feel a false sense of achievement simply because they had "made it to the gym." Once there, you need to work hard so you can *honestly* feel good about yourself for having taken one step closer to achieving your goals. Rather than going back to the gym over and over again to try and make up for lost time, do it right the first time.

# Part III
# RECOMMENDED EXERCISES

This section provides you with every recommended weight-training exercise. You are given complete descriptions and pictures to ensure that you perform the exercises properly, safely, and effectively.

The numbers next to the exercises refer to their order of interchangeability, which is discussed in the following subsection. The muscles listed first after "prime movers" are the muscles that are being directly trained. Along with the descriptions are many helpful tips.

If you have any questions about anything in this book, be sure to e-mail **questions@sportsworkout.com** for help from certified personal trainers.

## Substituting Similar Exercises

Our weight-training specialists did the hard work for you by strategically designing your program; all you have to do is follow it. Sometimes, however, there may be a required exercise or two that you either cannot perform physically or for which you do not have the equipment to perform. Many people struggle to do certain body weight exercises such as pull-ups or dips. Others may not have access to certain weight-training equipment such as cable or leg press machines. For these reasons, the exercises are listed for you are in order of interchangeability. If there is an exercise in your routine that you are not able to perform, substitute an exercise with a corresponding number from the same section. This substitution will ensure that you are training the same muscle groups in a similarly effective manner.

# Chest Exercises

## Interchangeable Chest Exercises

**1 Barbell Bench Press**

**1 Dumbbell Bench Press**

**1 Pushups**

**2 Incline Barbell Bench Press**

**2 Incline Dumbbell Bench Press**

**3 Flyes**

**3 Incline Flyes**

**3 Cable Crossovers**

**Dips (can be interchanged with any chest, shoulder, or triceps exercise)**

> **Safety tip!** When using a cable machine do not lower the weights so low or fast that they hit the weight stack. This stops the fluid motion of the lift and can cause injuries.

## Barbell Bench Press

Prime movers: Chest, triceps, shoulders.

**Starting Position:** Lie on a flat bench with your feet flat on the floor. Keep your eyes directly below the bar and your hands shoulder width apart. Lift the bar off its supports until your arms are extended.

**Lift:**

**a.** Slowly lower the bar until it grazes you chest. The bar should come to a brief, complete stop.

**b.** Push the bar back to full extension with the bar directly in line with your chin.

*Tip: Do not arch your back to try and lift more weight because it can cause serious back problems.*

*Tip: A closer grip trains your inner chest and triceps well; a wider grip works your outer chest.*

## Dumbbell Bench Press

Prime movers: Chest, triceps, shoulders.

**Starting Position:** Lie on a flat bench with your feet flat on the floor. Hold the dumbbells with your arms extended.

**Lift:**

**a.** Slowly lower the dumbbells until you feel a comfortable stretch in your chest. The dumbbells should come to a brief, complete stop slightly below your chest.

**b.** Push the dumbbells back to full extension.

*Tip: Dumbbells allow you to bring the weight lower than barbells, training your chest over the entire range of motion in ways a barbell cannot.*

## Pushups

Prime movers: Chest, shoulders, triceps.

**Starting Position:** Lie face down on the floor with your back straight and palms on the floor, shoulder width apart, your legs locked, and your toes on the floor with your heels in the air.

**Lift:**

**a.** Push your body upward off of the floor until your arms are fully extended.

**b.** Slowly lower yourself until your chest is about an inch from the floor with your legs remaining locked. Come to a brief, complete stop before continuing.

*Tip: To really train your triceps well, put your hands together and form a triangle with your index fingers and thumbs.*

## Incline Barbell Bench Press

Prime movers: Upper chest, triceps, shoulders.

**Starting Position**: Lie on an inclined bench with your feet flat on the floor. Keep your eyes directly below the bar and your hands shoulder width apart.

**Lift:** Lift the bar off of its supports until your arms are extended.

**a.** Slowly lower the bar until it grazes your chest. The bar should come to a brief, complete stop.

**b.** Push the bar back to full extension with the bar directly in line with your chin.

*Tip: You will not be able to lift as much as with a regular bench press. The steeper the degree of an incline, the less weight one typically is able to lift.*

### Incline Dumbbell Bench Press

Prime movers: Upper chest, triceps, shoulders.

**Starting Position:** Lie on an inclined bench with your feet flat on the floor. Hold the dumbbells with your arms extended in the starting position.

**Lift:**

**a.** Slowly lower the dumbbells until you feel a comfortable stretch in your chest. The dumbbells should come to a brief, complete stop slightly below your chest.

**b.** Push the dumbbells back to full extension.

### Flyes

Prime movers: Chest.

**Starting Position:** Lie on a bench with your feet flat on the floor. Hold the dumbbells with your arms extended and your palms facing each other so that the dumbbells are touching.

**Lift:**

**a.** Slowly lower the dumbbells away from each other with your arms slightly bent. Extend the dumbbells as wide as you can until you feel a comfortable stretch in your chest.

**b.** The dumbbells should come to a brief, complete stop slightly below your chest with your palms facing upward. Use your chest muscles to bring the dumbbells back to the starting position the same way they were brought down.

*Tip: As you bring the dumbbells together, rotating your wrists and touching the tops and bottoms of the dumbbells together is a nice change of pace and trains your muscles from different angles.*

### Incline Flyes

Prime movers: Chest

**Starting Position:** Lie on an inclined bench with your feet flat on the floor. Hold the dumbbells with your arms extended and your palms facing each other so that the dumbbells are touching.

**Lift:**

**a.** Slowly lower the dumbbells away from each other with your arms slightly bent. Extend the dumbbells as wide as you can until you feel a comfortable stretch in your chest.

**b.** The dumbbells should come to a brief, complete stop slightly below your chest with your palms facing upward. Use your chest muscles to bring the dumbbells back to the starting position the same way they were brought down.

## Cable Crossovers

Prime movers: Chest.

**Starting Position:** Stand bent slightly forward with your back straight and, with cables on both sides and slightly behind you, grab hold of the cables.

**Lift:**

**a.** With your arms slightly bent, use your chest to slowly bring the cables towards each other where they will pass each other in front of you. Cross the cables as far as you can.

**b.** The cables should come to a brief, complete stop. Then, slowly allow the cables to go back to the starting position the same way they were brought across.

*Tip: Alternate which arm is on top and bottom for every rep to ensure both sides are getting equal training.*

## Dips

Prime movers: Chest, shoulders, triceps.

**Starting Position:** With arms extended, grip the parallel bars with both hands so that your body is elevated off the floor.

**Lift:**

**a.** With your elbows tucked in as closely as possible and your back straight, slowly lower yourself until your chin is parallel with the bars.

**b.** Use your chest muscles, shoulders, and triceps to push back up to full extension with your arms locked.

*Tip: The farther you lean your body forward, the more your chest gets trained. As you straighten your body, your triceps begin to do the bulk of the work.*

# Back (Lats) Exercises

## Interchangeable Back (Lats) Exercises

**1 Lat Pull Downs**

**1 Behind-the-Neck Pull Downs**

**1 Seated Cable Rows**

**1 Pull-ups**

**2 Bent-Over Barbell Rows**

**2 Bent-Over Dumbbell Rows**

**2 T-bar Rows**

**2 One-Arm Dumbbell Rows**

### Lat Pull Downs

Prime movers: Lats, biceps, shoulders.

**Starting Position:** Sit at a lat pull down machine. Keep your back straight and lean backward a few inches with your feet resting on the floor. Grab the bar with both hands, using an overhand grip.

**Lift:**

**a.** Keeping your body stationary and bending at the elbows, pull the bar down in front of your neck, squeezing your shoulder blades together until the bar grazes your chest.

**b.** Let the bar come to a brief, complete stop before slowly and controllably guiding it back up to its original starting position, the same way you pulled it down.

*Tip: This exercise can also be performed with an underhand grip.*

**Tip for all pull-downs and pull-ups:** The wider the grip, the more you train the upper part of your back. The closer the grip, the more you train the lower part of your back.

## Behind-the-Neck Pull Downs:

Prime movers: Lats, shoulders, biceps.

**Starting Position:** Sit upright at a lat pull down machine. Keep your back straight with your feet resting on the floor. Grab the bar with both hands, using an overhand grip.

**Lift:**

**a.** Keeping your body stationary and bending at the elbows, pull the bar down behind your neck, squeeze your shoulder blades together, and bring the bar as low as you can.

**b.** Let the bar come to a brief, complete stop before slowly and controllably guiding it back up to its original starting position, the same way you pulled it down.

*Tip: More flexible people will be able to pull the bar down lower. Do not pull the bar down so low that it starts to feel uncomfortable. If you feel any unusual pain, DO NOT perform this exercise.*

## Seated Cable Rows

Prime movers: Lats, biceps, shoulders.

**Starting Position:**

Sit at a row machine with your back straight, feet resting on the foot rests and legs slightly bent. Lean forward and grab the handles.

**Lift:**

**a.** Keeping your back straight, lean backward and pull the handles towards your stomach as far back as you can, squeezing your shoulder blades together.

**b.** Let the handles come to a brief, complete stop before slowly and controllably guiding them back up to their original starting position, the same way you pulled them up.

## Pull-ups

Prime movers: Lats, biceps, shoulders.

**Starting Position:** Grab hold of a pull-up bar using an overhand grip with your arms completely extended and feet crossed and off the floor.

**Lift:**

**a.** Keeping your body stationary, feet crossed, and bending at the elbows, pull your body up in front of the bar as high as you can, squeezing your shoulder blades together.

**b.** Let your body come to a brief, complete stop before slowly and controllably lowering it back down to its original starting position, the same way you pulled it up.

*Tip: This exercise can also be performed behind the neck or with an underhand grip.*

*Tip: To train for optimal results, be sure to lower yourself all the way until your arms are nearly extended.*

## Bent-Over Barbell Rows

Prime movers: Lats, biceps, shoulders.

**Starting Position:** Standing with your knees slightly bent, feet a couple of inches apart, and bending at the waist to form an approximate ninety-degree angle, hold a bar with your arms hanging in front of you. Keep your back straight and your head tilted back.

**Lift:**

**a.** Keeping your body stationary and bending at the elbows, pull the bar up towards your stomach squeezing your shoulder blades together.

**b.** Let the bar come to a brief, complete stop before slowly and controllably guiding it back up to its original starting position, the same way you pulled it up.

*Tip for all bent-over back exercises: Do not pull the weights towards your chest; this does not isolate your lats as well as raising the bar to your stomach.*

## Bent-Over Dumbbell Rows

Prime movers: Lats, biceps, shoulders.

**Starting Position:** Standing with your knees slightly bent, feet a couple of inches apart, and bending at the waist to form an approximate ninety-degree angle, hang your arms to the sides and hold two dumbbells with your palms facing each other. Keep your back straight and your head tilted back.

**Lift:**

**a.** Keeping your body stationary and bending at the elbows, pull the dumbbells up the sides of your body as high as you can, squeezing your shoulder blades together.

**b.** Let the dumbbells come to a brief, complete stop before slowly and controllably guiding them back up to their original starting position, the same way you pulled them up.

## T-bar Rows

Prime movers: Lats, biceps, shoulders.

Starting Position: Standing with your knees slightly bent, feet a couple of inches apart, and bending at the waist to form a forty-five-degree angle with your floor, use an overhand grip to hold the handles of a T-bar machine, keeping the weights off of the floor. Keep your back straight and your head tilted back.

### Lift:

**a.** Keeping your body stationary and bending at the elbows, pull the bar up towards your chest squeezing your shoulder blades together.

**b.** Let the bar come to a brief, complete stop before slowly and controllably guiding it back up to its original starting position, the same way you pulled it up.

*Tip: If no T-bar machines are available, you can make your own using a barbell and a cable bar, as shown in the picture.*

## One-Arm Dumbbell Rows

Prime movers: Lats, biceps, shoulders.

**Starting Position:** Standing with your left hand and left knee resting on a bench, bend at the waist to form an approximate ninety-degree angle. Hang your right arm to the side and hold the dumbbell with your palm facing towards your body. Keep your back straight and your head tilted back.

### Lift:

**a.** Keeping your body stationary and bending at the elbow, pull the dumbbell up the side of your body as high as you can.

**b.** Let the dumbbell come to a brief, complete stop before slowly and controllably guiding it back up to its original starting position, the same way you pulled it up.

# Shoulders Exercises

## Interchangeable Shoulder Exercises

1 Barbell Military (Shoulder) Press

1 Dumbbell Military (Shoulder) Press

1 Push Press (Jerks)

2 Front Raises

2 Lateral Raises

2 Bent-Over Lateral Raises

2 Cable Lateral Raises

3 Standing Flyes

3 Upright Rows

4 Barbell Shrugs

4 Dumbbell Shrugs

5 Rotator Cuff Prone Position

5 Rotator Cuff On Side

### Barbell Military (Shoulder) Press

Prime movers: Shoulders, triceps.

**Starting Position:** Stand or sit upright and hold a bar at your shoulders, using an overhand grip. Grip the bar with your hands slightly wider than shoulder width.

**Lift:**

**a.** Keeping your body still, push the bar straight up until your arms are extended.

**b.** Slowly lower the bar down to the original starting position.

### Dumbbell Military (Shoulder) Press

Prime movers: Shoulders, triceps.

**Starting Position:** Stand or sit upright and hold dumbbells at your shoulders. Hold them with your hands slightly wider than shoulder width.

**Lift:**

**a.** Keeping your body still, push the dumbbells straight up until your arms are extended.

**b.** Slowly lower the dumbbells down to their original starting position.

## Push Press (Jerks)

Prime movers: Shoulders, triceps, legs.

**Starting Position:** Stand with your back straight and knees slightly bent. Hold the bar at your shoulders using an overhand grip. Grip the bar with your hands slightly wider than shoulder width.

**a.** Explode upwards with your legs to give the bar some upward momentum. With this momentum, push the bar straight up until your arms are extended.

**b.** Slowly lower the bar down and return to the starting position.

## Front Raises

Prime movers: Shoulders, traps.

Starting Position: Stand or sit upright and hold two dumbbells in front of you with your palms facing towards your body.

**Lift:**

**a.** With your arms remaining straight, raise the dumbbells out in front of you in one smooth, fluid motion until your hands are slightly above your shoulders.

**b.** Let the dumbbells come to a brief, complete stop before slowly lowering them back down to their original starting position, the same way you raised them up.

## Lateral Raises

Prime movers: Shoulders, traps.

**Starting Position:** Stand or sit upright and hold two dumbbells at your sides with your palms facing your body.

**Lift:**

**a.** With your arms remaining straight, raise the dumbbells out to your sides in one smooth, fluid motion until your hands are slightly above your shoulders

> **Tip for all shoulder raises:** Once you raise your arms beyond a ninety-degree angle with your body, you begin to focus more on your traps.

and slightly in front of you. As they reach this position, rotate your thumbs downward as if you are pouring a glass of water.

**b.** Let the dumbbells come to a brief, complete stop before slowly lowering them back down to their original starting position, the same way you raised them up.

*Tip: This exercise can also be performed with your palms pointing upward towards the ceiling.*
*Tip for all shoulder raises: You can raise the dumbbells with both arms at the same time or alternate arms.*

## Bent-Over Lateral Raises

Prime movers: Shoulders, traps.

**Starting Position:** Stand or sit bent at the waist, keeping your back completely straight and forming a ninety-degree angle with your legs. Let your arms hang straight down in front of you with your palms facing each other.

**Lift:**

**a.** With your arms remaining straight, raise your arms out to your sides until they are parallel with your shoulders and slightly in front of you. As they reach shoulder level, rotate your thumbs downward in one smooth, fluid motion as if you are pouring a glass of water.

**b.** Let the dumbbells come to a brief, complete stop before slowly lowering them back down to their original starting position the same way you raised them up.

## Cable Lateral Raises

Prime movers: Shoulders, traps.

**Starting Position:** Stand with your right arm next to a cable machine with your back straight. Grab hold of the cable with your left arm, so that your arm is hanging, slightly bent, across the front of your body. Rest the hand you are not using on your hip.

**Lift:**

**a.** Keeping your body still and your arm slightly bent, raise the cable across your body and out to the side in one motion until your hand is elevated slightly above your shoulder. As it reaches this level, rotate your thumbs downward in one smooth, fluid motion as if you are pouring a glass of water.

**b.** Let the cable come to a brief, complete stop before slowly lowering it back down to its original starting position the same way you raised it up.

## Standing Flyes

Prime movers: Shoulders, traps.

**Starting Position:**   Stand upright or with your knees slightly bent and bend at the waist with your back straight to form a forty-five-degree angle with your lower body.  With your palms facing each other, hold two dumbbells a few inches in front of your chest with your elbows bent at ninety-degree angles.

**Lift:**

**a.** Keeping your body still and your arms bent at 90-degree angles, pull the weights upward and backward as far back as you can, squeezing your shoulder blades together.

**b.** Come to a brief, complete stop before slowly returning the weights back to their starting position the same way you raised them up.

> **Tip for standing flyes and upright rows:** Avoid using your back and body momentum to complete these lifts because doing so is not an effective way of training and could cause injury.

## Upright Rows

Prime movers: Shoulders, traps, biceps.

**Starting Position:**   Stand   upright with  your  arms  hanging  in  front of  you.    Hold  a  barbell  with  an overhand grip.  Your hands should be roughly eight inches apart.

**Lift:**

**a.** Keeping your body still and back straight, raise the bar upwards to your chin, keeping the bar as close to your body as you can without touching it.

**b.** Let the bar come to a brief, complete stop before slowly lowering it back down to its original starting position the same way you raised it up.

## Barbell Shrugs

Prime movers: Traps

**Starting Position:** Stand upright  with your arms hanging in front of you. Hold a barbell with an overhand grip, hands roughly shoulder-width apart.

**Lift:**

**a.** Keeping your body still, back straight, and arms hanging in front of you, raise only your shoulders straight up.

**b.** Hold the position for at least three seconds before slowly lowering your shoulders back down to the original starting position.

## Dumbbell Shrugs

> **Tip for barbell and dumbbell shrugs:** Keeping your head down increases your range of motion for these exercises, giving your traps a better workout.

Prime movers: Traps

**Starting Position:** Stand upright with arms hanging at your sides. Hold dumbbells with your palms facing each other.

**Lift:**

**a.** Keeping your body still, back straight, and arms hanging at your sides, raise only your shoulders straight up.

**b.** Hold the position for at least three seconds before slowly lowering your shoulders back down to the original starting position.

## Rotator Cuff Prone Position

Area trained: Rotator cuff.

**Starting Position:**

Lie face down on a bench with one arm extended to the side so that your upper arm is parallel to the floor. Bend your arm at a ninety-degree angle so that your hand is hanging with your palm facing behind you. Hold a light weight in that hand.

**Lift:**

**a.** Keeping everything else stationary, rotate your forearm upward until it becomes parallel with the ground.

**b.** Slowly lower the weight back to its original starting position, the same way you brought it up.

> **Tip:** All rotator cuff exercises should always be performed very slowly and smoothly, and the weights for these exercises should **NEVER** exceed three lbs. or injuries will occur.

### Rotator Cuff on Side

Area trained: Rotator cuff.

**Starting Position:**

Lie on your side on a bench with your upper arm resting on your chest, parallel to the floor, and bent at the elbow at a ninety-degree angle so that your hand is hanging. Hold a light weight in that hand.

**Lift:**

**a.** Keeping everything else stationary, rotate your arm upward until it becomes parallel with the ground.

**b.** Slowly lower the weight back to its original starting position, the same way you brought it up.

# Triceps Exercises

**Interchangeable Triceps Exercises**

**1 Triceps Push Downs**

**1 Triceps Pull Downs**

**1 Skull Crushers**

**1 Triceps Kickbacks**

**1 Bench Dips**

**2 Barbell Triceps Curls**

**2 Dumbbell Triceps Curls**

**2 One-Arm Triceps Extensions**

### Triceps Push Downs

Prime movers: Triceps.

**Starting Position:** Stand or kneel with your back straight in front of a cable machine. Grab the bar with an overhand grip. Keep your elbows tucked in at your sides and hold the bar up by your chin.

**Lift:**

**a.** Keeping your body still and elbows tucked at your sides, push the bar straight down until your arms are fully extended.

**b.** Come to a brief, complete stop before slowly allowing the bar to rise back up to the starting position, with your elbows remaining tucked at your sides at all time.

*Tip: For variation, you can use many types of bars, including one-arm handles.*

### Triceps Pull Downs

This exercise is identical to triceps push downs with an underhand grip.

### Skull Crushers

Prime movers: Triceps.

**Starting Position:** Lie on a bench with your head partially hanging off the end. Hold a barbell with a close overhand grip straight out in front of you, above your forehead, with your arms extended.

**Lift:**

**a.** Keeping your body still and elbows motionless, slowly lower your forearms and the barbell down behind your head as far as you can.

**b.** Come to a brief, complete stop before returning the barbell to the starting position the same way you brought it down. Keep your elbows in and do not use your shoulders.

*Tip: If having your head partially off of the bench feels awkward and difficult, then perform this exercise with your head resting on the bench.*

> If balance becomes an issue while performing any cable machine triceps exercise, stand stagger stepped, with one leg behind the other.

## Triceps Kickbacks

Prime movers: Triceps.

**Starting Position:** Stand bending at the waist so your upper body is parallel with the floor with your knees slightly bent. Stand stagger stepped or place one knee on a bench and place your opposite hand on a bench for balance. With your elbow tucked in at your side and your upper arm also parallel to the floor, let your lower arm hang down perpendicular to the floor.

**Lift:**

**a.** Keeping your body still and elbow motionless, raise your lower arm backward until your arm is fully extended.

**b.** Come to a brief, complete stop before slowly lowering the dumbbell to the starting position, the same way you brought it up. Keep your elbow in and do not use your shoulder.

## Bench Dips:

Prime movers: Triceps, shoulders.

**Starting Position:** Place your heels on one bench in front of you and your palms on another bench behind you shoulder-width, leaving your rear hanging in the air. Your heels should be together and your hands should be shoulder-width apart. Your arms should be extended so that your body is elevated.

**Lift:**

**a.** Slowly lower yourself by bending at the elbows as low as you can by keeping the elbows tucked in as much as possible and keeping your back straight.

**b.** Push yourself back up to full extension with your arms locked.

*Tip: If your body weight alone is not providing enough resistance for a good workout, try placing some weights on your lap.*

## Barbell Triceps Curls

Prime movers: Triceps.

**Starting Position:** Stand or sit upright and hold a barbell above your head with your arms locked out and your elbows close to your head.

**Lift:**

**a.** Keeping your body still and elbows fixed close to your head, slowly lower your forearms and the bar down behind your head as far as you can.

**b.** Come to a brief, complete stop before returning the bar to the starting position, the same way you brought it down. Keep your elbows in and do not use your shoulders.

*Tip: Keeping your elbows in close to your head is sometimes difficult to do, but it ensures the best triceps workout.*

## Dumbbell Triceps Curls:

Prime movers: Triceps.

**Starting Position:** Stand or sit upright and hold a dumbbell above your head with both hands, your arms locked out, and your elbows close to your head.

**Lift:**

**a.** Keeping your body still and elbows fixed close to your head, slowly lower your forearms and the dumbbell down as far as you can.

**b.** Come to a brief, complete stop before returning the dumbbell to the starting position, the same way you brought it down. Keep your elbows in and do not use your shoulders.

## One-Arm Triceps Extensions:

Prime movers: Triceps.

**Starting Position:** Stand or sit upright and hold a dumbbell above your head with one hand. Keep your arm locked out and your elbow close to your head.

**Lift:**

**a.** Keeping your body still and elbow fixed close to your head, slowly lower your forearm and the dumbbell down behind your head as far as you can.

**b.** Come to a brief, complete stop before returning the dumbbell to the starting position, the same way you brought it down. Keep your elbow in and do not use your shoulder.

# Biceps/Forearms Exercises

## Interchangeable Biceps/ Forearms Exercises

## 1 Barbell Curls

## 1 Dumbbell Curls

## 1 Preacher Curls

## 1 Incline Dumbbell Curls

## 1 Concentration Curls

## 2 Reverse Barbell Curls

## 2 Reverse Dumbbell Curls

## 2 Hammer Curls

## 3 Behind Back Wrist Curls

## 3 Reverse Wrist Curls

## Barbell Curls

Prime movers: Biceps.

**Starting Position:** Stand upright with your feet roughly shoulder-width apart. Hold a barbell with your palms facing away from your body and elbows tucked into your sides.

**Lift:**

**a.** Keeping your elbows tucked at your sides at all times, use your biceps to curl the bar upward as high as you can until it is just below your chin.

**b.** With your elbows still tucked at your sides, slowly lower the bar back to its original starting position.

*Tip: Performing cheat curls (allowing your body to rock backward slightly to gain momentum) with this exercise from time to time can be beneficial to gaining mass in the biceps. You MUST wear a weight-lifting belt if you perform cheat curls. .*

## Dumbbell Curls

Prime movers: Biceps.

**Starting Position:** Stand or sit upright and with your feet roughly shoulder-width apart, hold dumbbells with your palms facing away from your body and elbows tucked into your sides.

**Lift:**

**a.** Keeping your elbows tucked at your sides at all times, use your biceps to curl the dumbbells upward as high as you can. You can curl with both arms at the same time or alternate arms.

**b.** With your elbows still tucked at your sides, slowly lower the bar back to its original starting position.

**Tip for all dumbbell biceps exercises:** Rotating your wrists inward towards your body will add extra emphasis and will give your biceps an even greater peak.

## Preacher Curls

Prime movers: Biceps.

**Starting Position:** Sit at a preacher bench with your elbows resting on the bench shoulder-width apart. Grip the bar with your palms facing upward.

**Lift:**

**a.** With your elbows remaining stationary, use your biceps to curl the bar upward as high as you can towards your chin, where you should flex your biceps for extra emphasis.

**b.** Slowly lower the bar back to its original starting point with your arms full extended.

*Tip: A closer grip trains your outer biceps and a wider grip trains your inner biceps.*

## Incline Dumbbell Curls

Prime movers: Biceps.

**Starting Position:** Sit on an inclined bench with your elbows tucked at your sides and your arms fully extended. Grip the dumbbells with your palms facing upward.

**Lift:**

**a.** Keeping your elbows tucked at your sides at all times, use your biceps to curl the dumbbells upward as high as you can. You can curl with both arms at the same time or alternate arms.

**b.** With your elbows still tucked at your sides, slowly lower the bar back to its original starting position.

## Concentration Curls

Prime movers: Biceps.

**Starting Position:** Sit on a bench slightly bent forward with your left arm gripping a dumbbell hanging between your legs. Your left palm should face your right leg and your right arm should rest on your knee.

**Lift:**

**a.** Keeping your elbow and upper arm stationary, curl the weight upward towards your shoulder.

**b.** With your elbow and upper arm still stationary, slowly lower the bar back to its original starting position.

## Reverse Barbell Curls

Prime movers: Forearms, biceps.

**Starting Position:** Stand upright with your feet roughly shoulder-width apart. Hold a barbell with your palms towards your body, your wrists locked, and elbows tucked into your sides.

**Lift:**

**a.** Keeping your elbows tucked at

your sides and wrists locked at all times, use your forearms and biceps to curl the bar upward as high as you can or until it is just below your chin.

**b.** With your elbows still tucked at your sides, slowly lower the bar back to its original starting position.

*Tip: Keeping your wrists locked adds extra emphasis to your forearms and ensures a great workout.*

## Reverse Dumbbell Curls

Prime movers: Forearms, biceps.

**Starting Position:** Stand or sit upright with your feet roughly shoulder-width apart. Hold two dumbbells with your palms facing towards your body, your wrists locked, and elbows tucked into your sides.

**Lift:**

**a.** Keeping your elbows tucked at your sides and wrists locked at all times, use your forearms and biceps to curl the dumbbells upward as high as you can. You can curl with both arms at the same time or alternate arms.

**b.** With your elbows still tucked at your sides and wrists locked, slowly lower the bar back to its original starting position.

## Hammer Curls

Prime movers: Forearms, biceps.

**Starting Position:** Stand or sit upright with your feet roughly shoulder-width apart. Hold two dumbbells with your palms facing each other, your wrists locked, and elbows tucked into your sides.

**Lift:**

**a.** Keeping your elbows tucked at your sides, wrists locked, and palms facing each other at all times, use your forearms and biceps to curl the dumbbells upward as high as you can. You can curl with both arms at the same time or alternate arms.

**b.** With your elbows still tucked at your sides, wrists locked, and palms facing each other, slowly lower the dumbbells back to their original starting position.

## Behind Back Wrist Curls

Prime movers: Forearms.

**Starting Position:** Stand upright with your feet roughly shoulder-width apart. Hold a barbell behind your back as if you are handcuffed with your palms facing away from your body and elbows tucked into your sides.

**Lift:**

**a.** Keeping your elbows tucked at your sides at all times, use your wrists to curl the bar upward towards your forearms.

**b.** With your elbows still tucked at your sides, slowly lower the bar with your wrists back to its original starting position.

### Reverse Wrist Curls

Prime movers: Forearms.

**Starting Position:** Sit at the end of a bench. Hold a barbell with an overhand grip with your palms facing the floor and your forearms resting on your thighs.

**Lift:**

**a.** Keeping everything stationary, use your wrists to curl the bar backwards as far as you can.

**b.** Slowly lower the bar with your wrists, back to its original starting position.

# Legs Exercises

**Interchangeable Leg Exercises**

**1 Squats**

**1 Leg Press**

**1 Dead Lift**

**1 Leg Extensions**

**1 Leg Curls**

**2 Standing Calf Raises**

**2 Seated Calf Raises**

**2 Reverse Calf Raises**

**3 Jump Squats**

**3 Power Cleans**

**4 Box Steps**

**4 Lunges**

## Squats

Prime movers: Upper and lower legs.

**Starting Position:** Stand upright with your feet shoulder-width apart and a barbell resting behind your neck on your traps with your hands slightly wider than shoulder-width apart, using an overhand grip. Keep your back straight and your head tilted up.

**Lift:**

**a.** With your back remaining straight and your head tilted up, slowly lower the weight by bending your knees until the upper part of your legs is parallel with the floor.

**b.** Explode upward back to the starting position. The entire lift should be in one smooth, fluid motion.

**Tip for squats and dead lifts:** Standing up on your toes as high as you can and holding it for a second or so upon returning to the starting position is a great built-in calves workout.

## Leg Press

Prime movers: Upper and lower legs.

**Starting Position:** Sit in a leg press machine with your back straight. Place your hands on the handlebars and your feet on the support bar.

**Lift:**

**a.** With everything remaining still, slowly lower the weight by bending your knees as far as you can.

**b.** Explode upward back to the starting position. The entire lift should be in one smooth, fluid motion.

*Tip: By not lowering the weights down very far, you are able to lift more weights, but will not be training your legs through the entire range of motion.*

## Dead Lift:

Prime movers: Upper and lower legs.

**Starting Position:** Stand with your back straight, head tilted back, and leaning slightly forward at the waist. Bend your knees so you can grab a barbell with your arms fully extended.

**a.** Keeping your arms locked, push with your legs to an upright position. Your lower back will also be used, but try to concentrate on using only your legs to lift the bar off the floor.

**b.** Slowly lower the bar so that it comes a few inches from the floor, with your arms and back remaining straight and head tilted up.

*Tip: You may find this exercise easier to perform by gripping the bar with one hand using an overhand grip and the other hand using an underhand grip as shown in the pictures.*

## Leg Extensions

Prime movers: Quadraceps.

**Starting Position:** Sit with your back straight and hands gripping the handlebars in a leg-extension machine. Place your feet underneath the bar.

Lift:

**a.** With everything remaining still, raise the bar with your feet by extending your legs as far as you can.

**b.** Slowly lower your legs back down towards the starting position the same way you brought them up.

*Tip: If all of the weights on your leg extension/curl machine are still not enough for you, you can perform this exercise one leg at a time.*

## Leg Curls

Prime movers: Hamstrings.

**Starting Position:** With your back straight and hands gripping the handlebars, lie face down on a leg curl machine and place your feet underneath the bar.

Lift:

**a.** With everything remaining still, raise the bar with your feet by curling your legs as far as you can.

**b.** Slowly lower your legs towards the starting position the same way you brought them up.

### Standing Calf Raises

Prime movers: Calves.

**Starting Position:** Stand with your shoulders under the supports of a standing calf raise machine and your toes on the elevated stand provided so that your heels are hanging off the end. Keep your back straight and hands gripping the handlebars.

**a.** With everything remaining still, stand up on your toes as high as you can. Hold the position for a brief moment to maximize the work on your calves.

**b.** Slowly lower your heels back down towards the starting position the same way you brought them up.

*Tip for all calf raises: To ensure the best workout, raise and lower your heels as high and as low as you can, training your calves through the entire range of motion.*

### Seated Calf Raises

Prime movers: Calves.

**Starting Position:** Sit with your knees under the supports of a standing calf raise machine and your toes on the elevated stand provided so that your heels are hanging off of the stand. Keep your back straight and hands gripping the handlebars.

**a.** With everything remaining still, rise up on your toes as high as you can. Hold the position for a brief moment to maximize the work on your calves.

**b.** Slowly lower your heels back down towards the starting position the same way you brought them up.

### Reverse Calf Raises

Prime movers: Front of lower legs.

**Starting Position:** Stand upright with your heels on an elevated stand or block so that your toes are hanging off the stand. This exercise is best performed with no added resistance other than your body weight.

**a.** With everything remaining still, stand up on your heels as high as you can. Hold the position for a brief moment to maximize the work on the front of your lower legs.

**b.** Slowly lower your toes back down towards the starting position the same way you brought them up.

## Jump Squats

Prime movers: Upper and lower legs.

**Starting Position:** Stand in a squatting position with your feet shoulder-width apart and your arms crossed over your chest. Keep your back straight and your head tilted up.

**Lift:**

**a.** With everything remaining still, explosively jump straight up as high as you can.

**b.** As you land, return to the starting position in one smooth motion.

## Power Cleans

Prime movers: Upper and lower legs.

**Starting Position:** Stand with your back straight and head titled back. Lean slightly forward at the waist so your shoulders are in front of the bar on the floor. Keep your feet at least shoulder-width apart and your knees bent so you can grab a barbell with your arms fully extended, using an overhand grip.

**a.** Keeping your arms straight, push with your legs and raise the

bar up close to your body to your lower thigh with your knees still slightly bent.

**b.** From this point, use your lower body for momentum to push yourself straight up while simultaneously using your shoulders to raise the bar to your stomach.

**c.** In one explosive movement, flip your wrists and elbows underneath the bar while simultaneously jumping into a partial squatting position.

## Box Steps

Prime movers: Upper and lower legs.

**Starting Position:** Stand upright with your feet shoulder-width apart and a barbell resting behind your neck on your traps with your hands slightly wider than shoulder-width apart, using an overhand grip or holding dumbbells at your sides. Keep your back straight and your head tilted up. Stand with a box, bench, or some sort of elevated apparatus in front of you.

**a.** Step forward up on the box or bench with your right foot. Bring your left knee up so that your left thigh is parallel to the floor.

**b.** Lower your left leg all the way back down to the floor and bring your right leg back down to meet it. Repeat with other leg.

## Lunges

Prime movers: Upper and lower legs.

**Starting Position:** Stand upright with your feet together and either a barbell resting behind your neck on your traps or holding two dumbbells at your sides as in the picture. Your hands should be slightly wider than shoulder-width apart, using an overhand grip. Keep your back straight and your head tilted up.

**Lift:**

**a.** With everything remaining still, slowly take a large step forward with one leg, bending both knees. The weight on your back foot should come up on your toes, and the knee on your back leg should come very close, but not touch the floor.

**b.** Using your extended leg, thrust yourself back to the starting position the same way you came down. The entire lift should be in one smooth, fluid motion.

*Tip: The longer your step forward, the more effective this exercise will be.*

# Part IV
# THE NECESSITIES

## Perfecting Your Technique

This section identifies what you need to accomplish before you begin the program. The information in this section is extremely important for beginners and is also important for experienced weight trainers who have never performed some of the recommended exercises. To follow any type of weight-training routine, you first need to get a feel for the weight room and learn your own strengths.

Now is the time to test out your form, style, and technique. Be sure to take a day or so to perform warm-up sets with each of the exercises listed in that specific program. The object of these first few sessions is not to train so hard that you are sore the following days, but to practice your form and to gain an understanding for yourself and for the weight room. Simply go to the gym with this book, read the recommended exercises section, and go through a few reps of each exercise using very light weights.

These initial days of practice are very important and can be a major help to you as you progress as a weight trainer and athlete by helping you gain an understanding of approximately how much weight you can handle for each exercise.

# Estimating Your One Rep Max

> **Your one rep max** is the greatest amount of weight you can lift one time or for one repetition for a particular exercise.

Knowing your one rep max is an essential part of measuring your strength, your progress, and is very helpful in determining the weight load you should be lifting for every set, regardless of your purpose. This section is called *Estimating* Your One Rep Max because this book never recommends that you *max out*. As discussed in earlier sections, *maxing out* can cause injuries, which, besides being painful and dangerous, can prevent future weight training. *Auxiliary exercises*, or exercises training smaller muscle groups such as biceps and forearms, can be particularly dangerous when trying to max out. With the estimated one rep max chart provided for you, you can estimate your one rep max without having to attempt to lift your max weight. Instead, you can lift a lighter weight several times to safely and accurately estimate what your max is.

Your estimated one rep max for each exercise is an underlying foundation for weight training. All of the sets and reps you are required to perform are based on percentages of your estimated one rep max.

## Understanding the Chart
### Steps to finding your estimated one rep max:

1. Choose an exercise that you want to try to find your estimated one rep max.
2. Choose a test weight that is light enough for you to lift several, but not more than, eight times.
3. Lift that weight until failure. If you lift more than eight reps, choose a higher weight and start over.
4. Find your test weight on the far left column of the Estimated One-Rep Max Chart.
5. Find the number of reps you successfully completed on the top row.
6. Scroll right from your test weight and down from your successfully completed reps until you find the number that shares both the same row and column.

**The number you arrive at is your estimated one rep max.**

> For an easier way of determining your one-rep max, log on to **www.sportsworkout.com** to use a **one-rep max calculator.**

# REPS

| WEIGHT | 1 | 2 | 3 | 4 | 5 | 6 | 7 | 8 |
|---|---|---|---|---|---|---|---|---|
| 5 | 5 | 5 | 5 | 6 | 6 | 6 | 6 | 6 |
| 10 | 10 | 10 | 11 | 11 | 11 | 12 | 12 | 12 |
| 15 | 15 | 15 | 16 | 16 | 17 | 17 | 18 | 19 |
| 20 | 20 | 21 | 21 | 22 | 23 | 23 | 24 | 25 |
| 25 | 25 | 26 | 27 | 27 | 28 | 29 | 30 | 31 |
| 30 | 30 | 31 | 32 | 33 | 34 | 35 | 36 | 37 |
| 35 | 35 | 36 | 37 | 38 | 39 | 41 | 42 | 44 |
| 40 | 40 | 41 | 42 | 44 | 45 | 47 | 48 | 50 |
| 45 | 45 | 46 | 48 | 49 | 51 | 52 | 54 | 56 |
| 50 | 50 | 51 | 53 | 55 | 56 | 58 | 60 | 62 |
| 55 | 55 | 57 | 58 | 60 | 62 | 64 | 66 | 68 |
| 60 | 60 | 62 | 64 | 66 | 68 | 70 | 72 | 75 |
| 65 | 65 | 67 | 69 | 71 | 73 | 76 | 78 | 81 |
| 70 | 70 | 72 | 74 | 76 | 79 | 81 | 84 | 87 |
| 75 | 75 | 77 | 79 | 82 | 84 | 87 | 90 | 93 |
| 80 | 80 | 82 | 85 | 87 | 90 | 93 | 96 | 99 |
| 85 | 85 | 87 | 90 | 93 | 96 | 99 | 102 | 106 |
| 90 | 90 | 93 | 95 | 98 | 101 | 105 | 108 | 112 |
| 95 | 95 | 98 | 101 | 104 | 107 | 110 | 114 | 118 |
| 100 | 100 | 103 | 106 | 109 | 113 | 116 | 120 | 124 |
| 105 | 105 | 108 | 111 | 115 | 118 | 122 | 126 | 130 |
| 110 | 110 | 113 | 117 | 120 | 124 | 128 | 132 | 137 |
| 115 | 115 | 118 | 122 | 126 | 129 | 134 | 138 | 143 |
| 120 | 120 | 123 | 127 | 131 | 135 | 139 | 144 | 149 |
| 125 | 125 | 129 | 132 | 136 | 141 | 145 | 150 | 155 |
| 130 | 130 | 134 | 138 | 142 | 146 | 151 | 156 | 161 |
| 135 | 135 | 139 | 143 | 147 | 152 | 157 | 162 | 168 |
| 140 | 140 | 144 | 148 | 153 | 158 | 163 | 168 | 174 |
| 145 | 145 | 149 | 154 | 158 | 163 | 168 | 174 | 180 |
| 150 | 150 | 154 | 159 | 164 | 169 | 174 | 180 | 186 |
| 155 | 155 | 159 | 164 | 169 | 174 | 180 | 186 | 193 |
| 160 | 160 | 165 | 169 | 175 | 180 | 186 | 192 | 199 |
| 165 | 165 | 170 | 175 | 180 | 186 | 192 | 198 | 205 |
| 170 | 170 | 175 | 180 | 186 | 191 | 197 | 204 | 211 |
| 175 | 175 | 180 | 185 | 191 | 197 | 203 | 210 | 217 |
| 180 | 180 | 185 | 191 | 196 | 203 | 209 | 216 | 224 |
| 185 | 185 | 190 | 196 | 202 | 208 | 215 | 222 | 230 |
| 190 | 190 | 195 | 201 | 207 | 214 | 221 | 228 | 236 |
| 195 | 195 | 201 | 207 | 213 | 219 | 227 | 234 | 242 |
| 200 | 200 | 206 | 212 | 218 | 225 | 232 | 240 | 248 |

# REPS

| WEIGHT | 1 | 2 | 3 | 4 | 5 | 6 | 7 | 8 |
|---|---|---|---|---|---|---|---|---|
| 205 | 205 | 211 | 217 | 224 | 231 | 238 | 246 | 255 |
| 210 | 210 | 216 | 222 | 229 | 236 | 244 | 252 | 261 |
| 215 | 215 | 221 | 228 | 235 | 242 | 250 | 258 | 267 |
| 220 | 220 | 226 | 233 | 240 | 248 | 256 | 264 | 273 |
| 225 | 225 | 231 | 238 | 246 | 253 | 261 | 270 | 279 |
| 230 | 230 | 237 | 244 | 251 | 259 | 267 | 276 | 286 |
| 235 | 235 | 242 | 249 | 256 | 264 | 273 | 282 | 292 |
| 240 | 240 | 247 | 254 | 262 | 270 | 279 | 288 | 298 |
| 245 | 245 | 252 | 259 | 267 | 276 | 285 | 294 | 304 |
| 250 | 250 | 257 | 265 | 273 | 281 | 290 | 300 | 310 |
| 255 | 255 | 262 | 270 | 278 | 287 | 296 | 306 | 317 |
| 260 | 260 | 267 | 275 | 284 | 293 | 302 | 312 | 323 |
| 265 | 265 | 273 | 281 | 289 | 298 | 308 | 318 | 329 |
| 270 | 270 | 278 | 286 | 295 | 304 | 314 | 324 | 335 |
| 275 | 275 | 283 | 291 | 300 | 309 | 319 | 330 | 341 |
| 280 | 280 | 288 | 297 | 306 | 315 | 325 | 336 | 348 |
| 285 | 285 | 293 | 302 | 311 | 321 | 331 | 342 | 354 |
| 290 | 290 | 298 | 307 | 316 | 326 | 337 | 348 | 360 |
| 295 | 295 | 303 | 312 | 322 | 332 | 343 | 354 | 366 |
| 300 | 300 | 309 | 318 | 327 | 338 | 348 | 360 | 373 |
| 305 | 305 | 314 | 323 | 333 | 343 | 354 | 366 | 379 |
| 310 | 310 | 319 | 328 | 338 | 349 | 360 | 372 | 385 |
| 315 | 315 | 324 | 334 | 344 | 354 | 366 | 378 | 391 |
| 320 | 320 | 329 | 339 | 349 | 360 | 372 | 384 | 397 |
| 325 | 325 | 334 | 344 | 355 | 366 | 378 | 390 | 404 |
| 330 | 330 | 339 | 349 | 360 | 371 | 383 | 396 | 410 |
| 335 | 335 | 345 | 355 | 366 | 377 | 389 | 402 | 416 |
| 340 | 340 | 350 | 360 | 371 | 383 | 395 | 408 | 422 |
| 345 | 345 | 355 | 365 | 376 | 388 | 401 | 414 | 428 |
| 350 | 350 | 360 | 371 | 382 | 394 | 407 | 420 | 435 |
| 355 | 355 | 365 | 376 | 387 | 399 | 412 | 426 | 441 |
| 360 | 360 | 370 | 381 | 393 | 405 | 418 | 432 | 447 |
| 365 | 365 | 375 | 387 | 398 | 411 | 424 | 438 | 453 |
| 370 | 370 | 381 | 392 | 404 | 416 | 430 | 444 | 459 |
| 375 | 375 | 386 | 397 | 409 | 422 | 436 | 450 | 466 |
| 380 | 380 | 391 | 402 | 415 | 428 | 441 | 456 | 472 |
| 385 | 385 | 396 | 408 | 420 | 433 | 447 | 462 | 478 |
| 390 | 390 | 401 | 413 | 426 | 439 | 453 | 468 | 484 |
| 395 | 395 | 406 | 418 | 431 | 444 | 459 | 474 | 490 |
| 400 | 400 | 411 | 424 | 436 | 450 | 465 | 480 | 497 |

# REPS

| WEIGHT | 1 | 2 | 3 | 4 | 5 | 6 | 7 | 8 |
|---|---|---|---|---|---|---|---|---|
| 405 | 405 | 417 | 429 | 442 | 456 | 470 | 486 | 503 |
| 410 | 410 | 422 | 434 | 447 | 461 | 476 | 492 | 509 |
| 415 | 415 | 427 | 439 | 453 | 467 | 482 | 498 | 515 |
| 420 | 420 | 432 | 445 | 458 | 473 | 488 | 504 | 522 |
| 425 | 425 | 437 | 450 | 464 | 478 | 494 | 510 | 528 |
| 430 | 430 | 442 | 455 | 469 | 484 | 499 | 516 | 534 |
| 435 | 435 | 447 | 461 | 475 | 489 | 505 | 522 | 540 |
| 440 | 440 | 453 | 466 | 480 | 495 | 511 | 528 | 546 |
| 445 | 445 | 458 | 471 | 486 | 501 | 517 | 534 | 553 |
| 450 | 450 | 463 | 477 | 491 | 506 | 523 | 540 | 559 |
| 455 | 455 | 468 | 482 | 496 | 512 | 529 | 546 | 565 |
| 460 | 460 | 473 | 487 | 502 | 518 | 534 | 552 | 571 |
| 465 | 465 | 478 | 492 | 507 | 523 | 540 | 558 | 577 |
| 470 | 470 | 483 | 498 | 513 | 529 | 546 | 564 | 584 |
| 475 | 475 | 489 | 503 | 518 | 534 | 552 | 570 | 590 |
| 480 | 480 | 494 | 508 | 524 | 540 | 558 | 576 | 596 |
| 485 | 485 | 499 | 514 | 529 | 546 | 563 | 582 | 602 |
| 490 | 490 | 504 | 519 | 535 | 551 | 569 | 588 | 608 |
| 495 | 495 | 509 | 524 | 540 | 557 | 575 | 594 | 615 |
| 500 | 500 | 514 | 529 | 546 | 563 | 581 | 600 | 621 |
| 505 | 505 | 519 | 535 | 551 | 568 | 587 | 606 | 627 |
| 510 | 510 | 525 | 540 | 556 | 574 | 592 | 612 | 633 |
| 515 | 515 | 530 | 545 | 562 | 579 | 598 | 618 | 639 |
| 520 | 520 | 535 | 551 | 567 | 585 | 604 | 624 | 646 |
| 525 | 525 | 540 | 556 | 573 | 591 | 610 | 630 | 652 |
| 530 | 530 | 545 | 561 | 578 | 596 | 616 | 636 | 658 |
| 535 | 535 | 550 | 567 | 584 | 602 | 621 | 642 | 664 |
| 540 | 540 | 555 | 572 | 589 | 608 | 627 | 648 | 671 |
| 545 | 545 | 561 | 577 | 595 | 613 | 633 | 654 | 677 |
| 550 | 550 | 566 | 582 | 600 | 619 | 639 | 660 | 683 |
| 555 | 555 | 571 | 588 | 606 | 624 | 645 | 666 | 689 |
| 560 | 560 | 576 | 593 | 611 | 630 | 650 | 672 | 695 |
| 565 | 565 | 581 | 598 | 616 | 636 | 656 | 678 | 702 |
| 570 | 570 | 586 | 604 | 622 | 641 | 662 | 684 | 708 |
| 575 | 575 | 591 | 609 | 627 | 647 | 668 | 690 | 714 |
| 580 | 580 | 597 | 614 | 633 | 653 | 674 | 696 | 720 |
| 585 | 585 | 602 | 619 | 638 | 658 | 679 | 702 | 726 |
| 590 | 590 | 607 | 625 | 644 | 664 | 685 | 708 | 733 |
| 595 | 595 | 612 | 630 | 649 | 669 | 691 | 714 | 739 |
| 600 | 600 | 617 | 635 | 655 | 675 | 697 | 720 | 745 |

# The Different Folks, Different Strokes Principle

As the title of this section indicates, not everyone is the same. In weight training, differences can occur both physically and psychologically. Some people are born with greater muscle-building capabilities than others. A major reason for these genetic differences is the amount of fast-twitch muscle fibers one has. Fast-twitch fibers are able to grow bigger and stronger than the other muscle fibers. Do not feel frustrated if you see others making faster initial gains than you are, because you can and will make enormous gains by following any one of the provided programs. By sticking with your routine and working hard, you can catch and surpass almost everyone. Fast-twitch, as well as slow-twitch fibers, are explained in further detail in the section Muscle Fibers.

## Overtraining and Staleness

**Overtraining** is when you work out so hard that your training negatively affects your goals.

Everyone, at one point or another, reaches a plateau in his or her training. When this happens, gains are very hard to come by. Many times plateaus occur because of overtraining. Overtraining can occur during one workout, or it can gradually creep up on you over time. It is important to push yourself as hard as you can in the gym and make the most of your time, but there can be a time when you are doing too much. Training seven days a week is an example of overtraining. We all need rest days so our muscles can recoup, regroup, and rebuild. It is during these days off that your body is able to grow bigger and stronger. Even the biggest and strongest athletes, body builders, and weight lifters take at least one day of rest per week.

> Your muscles need at least forty-eight hours to fully recover from weight training, which is why you should never train the same muscle groups on consecutive days.

During one session, some people are able to work out for hours without overtraining, while others simply can't handle that much physical stress. Most beginners will not be able to work out for as long or as often as more experienced weight trainers because their bodies are not yet prepared for that type of strenuous work.

Staleness, on the other hand, is thought by many experts to be a response to overtraining. It is a syndrome that negatively affects your athletic performance and your personality. Rest is the only method of prevention and the only cure for staleness. The program provided for you has been designed so that there is a minimal chance of overtraining and staleness occurring; however, if you do begin to notice symptoms, take at least one week off from weight training and see your physician.

## Symptoms of staleness include:

1. Reaching a plateau in training gains
2. Having unusual sleeping patterns
3. Performing tasks seems more difficult
4. Having a decreased appetite leading to unhealthy lean body weight loss
5. Having increased irritability and anxiety
6. Experiencing depression
7. Having a decreased sex drive

Endurance athletes are at the greatest risk of staleness; however, all athletes should be aware of this syndrome regardless of the sport. The different folks, different strokes principle applies to staleness. Many athletes may never experience staleness, but everyone needs to be aware that it can happen.

# The Declaration of Variation

Variation is introducing some sort of change in your workout routine. It can be the constant changing of exercises within a program or the compete changing of your program every few weeks. Variation is very important in weight training for several physiological and psychological reasons. Some of the most important benefits of variation in a weight-training program include:

1. **Not allowing your body to adapt to any one routine:** Perhaps the most important reason to vary your routines is so you can keep making progress and gains. Variation is the key to continued progress. Your body is a machine designed to adapt to any stress placed on it, whether it be heat, pressure, or tension. Similarly, your body adapts to the workload you are putting on it in the gym. After following the same routine for long enough, you will plateau because your body has become used to and has adapted to doing the same thing over and over again. When a plateau occurs, you need to shock your body with different types of stimuli to continue making gains. By occasionally switching the type of training you do (how many reps, sets, exercises, and their order), you shock your body so that it has to readapt to the new workload you are putting on it, which enables you to continue to progress.

2. **Keeping you from getting bored:** Following the same routine day after day can become very boring and tiresome. Fitness experts and coaches alike know that boredom in the gym can be a major problem for athletes and other weight trainers. In order to make big gains, you need to train hard and with intensity. Once that intensity is lost, so are the benefits from training hard. When people are bored with their routine, they lose motivation and train with less passion. It is human nature. Unfortunately, this lack of motivation spawns a negative cycle. By not training as hard, gains become more difficult, thus leading to an even greater decrease in motivation, which leads again to not training hard. And so the cycle continues. Varying exercises and styles every so often keeps things fresh and keeps people motivated, especially athletes in the midst of a long off-season.

**3. Targeting, strengthening, and toning every part of every muscle:** As you've noticed, this book provides you with many weight-training exercises. Many of these exercises train the same muscle groups. Like people, no two exercises are exactly alike. Some may be similar, but not identical. Each exercise targets your muscle from a different angle and achieves a different benefit. By using a variety of exercises on the same muscles, you strengthen every part of those muscles.

# Muscle Fibers
(How to Train, What and Why)

Our muscles are made up of many bundles of muscle fibers. Each fiber type has its own characteristics and purposes. For simplicity purposes, these muscle fibers can be categorized as:

1. **Fast-Twitch Fibers**
2. **Slow-Twitch Fibers**
3. **Intermediate Fibers (properties of both)**

The muscle-fiber makeup in most people is roughly 25% fast twitch, 25% slow twitch, and 50% intermediate fibers, which contain properties of both fast- and slow-twitch muscle fibers. With proper training some of the intermediate fibers can be converted to fast- or slow–twitch fibers. The more fast-twitch fibers one has, the more powerful and explosive he or she will be. People with more slow-twitch fibers will have greater endurance and stamina. Depending on your purpose, you can weight train in order to build up either muscle fiber.

## Fast-Twitch Fibers

Generally, fast-twitch fibers are used in strength and explosive sports or sports that require bursts of speed and power for relatively short amounts of time. A running back bursting through a hole, a baseball or softball player trying to beat out an infield hit, a basketball player exploding up to the hoop for a slam, a golfer ripping a drive three hundred yards off the tee, a tennis player smashing a backhand across the court, a short distance swimmer torpedoing through the water, and a 110 hurdler flying down the lane are all putting their fast-twitch fibers to the test. Any type of explosive movement is being performed by fast-twitch fibers. People who participate in these or similar types of activities should concentrate primarily on working their fast-twitch fibers

The simple reason more fast-twitch muscle fibers lead to better performance in explosive activities is because they contract faster and with more power than slow-twitch fibers. Fast-twitch fibers lead to *hypertrophy*—an increase in the size of muscle fibers as an outcome of weight training—more easily than slow-twitch fibers. As your muscle fibers increase in size, so do your muscles. The downside to fast-twitch fibers is that they can only work at full capacity for short periods of time before fatiguing because they work primarily without oxygen, or *anaerobically*, and get most of their energy from limited stores of muscle glycogen.

## Slow-Twitch Fibers

Slow-twitch fibers are used in stamina and endurance-based activities. Long distance runners, cyclists, swimmers, and triathletes are examples of people who should concentrate on slow-twitch training. Slow-twitch fibers contract more slowly than fast-twitch fibers, but are able to work for hours longer if trained properly. Slow-twitch fibers get their energy aerobically, from oxygen. Slow-twitch training is great for burning fat because oxygen stimulates the use of fat for energy. There is less hypertrophy in slow-twitch fibers, which is why marathon runners tend to be much smaller than football players.

# Training Techniques

**Training to Failure:** Training to failure means training in a particular set until you exhaust yourself and cannot complete another repetition on your own. Whether you are training for endurance, power, or strength, it is recommended that you train to failure in most of your sets. By training to failure, you train your body to its maximum capabilities. This type of training is tough, but well worth the results.

**Forced Reps:** Forced reps are performed directly after you have trained to positive failure and cannot complete another repetition. You lower the weight regularly and your partner helps you slowly lift it back up. Your partner should assist you to complete the rep, but not do all of the work for you. Your partner should make sure you spend at least three or four seconds on the positive phase of the lift while assisting you.

**Negatives:** Negatives are also performed directly after you have trained to failure. The opposite of forced reps, the eccentric, or lowering aspect of the lift, is extremely slow, and the concentric part of the lift is fast, with the help of your partner. It should take you approximately six or seven seconds to lower the weights with the help of your partner. At this point, with the help from a spotter, quickly return the weights to their starting position and repeat. Using negatives is the best method for increasing strength and size; however, they should not be used very often because they work your muscles so hard they need over a week in order to fully recover before performing them again.

**Supersets:** This is a training method where you perform one set of two exercises sequentially without rest. For example, if you were to superset preacher curls with triceps curls, you would do one set of preachers and immediately after completion, do one set of triceps curls and then rest before repeating.

> You are able to perform negatives with weights higher than your one rep max because eccentrically you can lift a great deal more than you can concentrically.

**Tri Sets:**  Same as Supersets but with three exercises instead of two.

**Pre-exhaust:**  This method is one of the most intense methods of weight training.  It is a form of supersetting where you perform many reps of a single-joint exercise and immediately follow it up with a compound exercise training the same muscles.  For example, if you were to pre-exhaust your shoulders, you would first perform many reps of light lateral raises and immediately follow it up with a military press.

**Burnouts (stripping method):**  This method is very popular and very effective.  Directly after you complete a set working to failure, immediately lighten the load of the weights so you can continue to train without rest, and perform the next set to failure where you will again lighten the load and work to failure.

**Pyramid Method:**  The pyramid method is a great strength-building tactic.  It is performed properly by decreasing the reps and increasing the weight with every set.  An example would be performing five reps with 100 lbs. followed by three reps with 120 lbs. and one rep with 140 lbs.

**21's:**  This method is most often performed for biceps exercises, particularly for preacher curls.  These exercises are properly executed by performing seven reps going from the bottom of the lift to the halfway point and back for seven reps, then performing seven reps going from the halfway point to the top, followed by seven reps through the complete range of motion.

**Cycling:**  Cycling is rotating between two or three different routines.  As long as the routines are different, it is considered cycling.  A holistic cycle would be following an endurance program, then a power program, and then a strength program.  It is best to take one week of active or complete rest after you have completed a full cycle to let your body completely recover before beginning again.  Active rest is any sort of low-level, non-structured activity.

**Circuit Training:**  Circuit training is the best method of weight training for total fitness and aerobic benefits.  It is a great way to get a fast and effective full-body workout.  Circuit training is a type of endurance training in which you perform one set of six to ten exercises consecutively without rest. The six to ten exercises should train the major muscle groups of your entire body for a complete workout. After you have completed one circuit through the entire rotation, rest for a short time before repeating.

# When to Increase
## (The X + 3 Method)

> **Rule of thumb:** Increase the number of reps before increasing the weight.

The goal of weight training is to gradually increase the resistance over time. Two ways of increasing the resistance are:

1. **Increasing the weight**
2. **Increasing the number of reps**

Increasing the weight you lift can be overwhelming and difficult, so this book recommends that once a weight begins to feel too light for the designated number of repetitions, increase the number of reps before increasing the weight. The X + 3 method states that if you are required to lift X reps in a given set and are able to accomplish it, then the next time you lift, go for X + 1 reps using the same weight. As each exercise begins to feel lighter and lighter, increase your reps up until X + 3. When reps of X + 3 become easily attainable, increase the weight by 5 lbs. and return to reps of X, repeating this entire process. While training smaller, auxiliary-muscle groups like your biceps, triceps and forearms, make increases by 2 pounds at a time. Below is an example of the X + 3 method.

> Your routine requires you to bench 100 lbs. 10 times. You complete the 10 reps with ease and the next time you go to the gym you lifts 100 lbs. 11 times. You continue this process until benching 100 lbs. 13 times becomes easy. At this point, you increase your bench to 105 lbs. and start back with 10 reps.

# Safety Reminders

When done properly, weight training can be a very effective way to sculpt your body and achieve your athletic potential. On top of all of the performance-enhancing benefits to weight training, it also plays a major role in injury reduction, injury prevention, and injury rehabilitation. With stronger muscles supporting your bones, tendons, and ligaments, you will be much less injury prone and will able to perform most activities hard and strong all the time. However, if necessary safety precautions are not followed, injuries can result.

**Listed below are a few safety reminders to help keep you injury free in the gym.**

**Always use a spotter:** It does not matter how experienced you are or how light you think the weight is, you always need someone to spot you.

**Use safety collars:** Collars will prevent weights from tipping over during a lift, which can result in an injury to you or others.

**Pick up weights properly:** Most injuries in the weight room come from picking up and putting weights down improperly. To avoid chronic lower-back problems, be sure to bend at the knees and to keep your back straight every time you pick up or put down weights.

**Drink enough water:** Even if you are not thirsty, be sure to drink lots of water before and during your workout, especially if you anticipate a lot of perspiration. As you become dehydrated, your ability to perform work drops way off, which will limit your intensity and slow your progress.

**Use proper form:** Proper form will provide you with the best results and help keep you injury free.

**Breathe correctly:** It is very important to simply breathe while performing any exercise, inhaling on the negative part of the lift and exhaling on the positive part. Do not hold your breath! .

**Do not drop weights:** Not only can this break the weights, but it can also be very dangerous for everyone in the gym. Always put the weights back in a controlled manner.

**Dress properly:** Gym shoes are a must; wearing inappropriate gym attire like sandals can results in injuries such as broken toes.

**Use your head:** If you begin to feel sick, queasy, light-headed, or if you experience joint or chest pains, stop your session and get yourself checked out immediately.

**Consult your physician:** It is required for everyone to check with his or her physician before beginning any one of the prescribed programs or before increasing the intensity to any of the programs.

# Record Keeping

When following any type of program, it is vital that you keep daily records for many reasons. Five of the most important are:

1.  **Knowing when to increase the weight or reps**
2.  **Knowing where to start after taking time away from the gym**
3.  **Observing your gains over time**
4.  **Motivation**
5.  **Detect overtraining**

You can keep records on any or all of a vast number of factors that may be important to your training or progress. You have been provided with an example of a record-keeping chart to help you monitor your progress. You can print an unlimited amount of these charts from **www.sportsworkout.com/chart.htm.** They have been made accessible so you can keep records in the very best and easiest way possible. To complement the record-keeping chart, there is a *testing sheet*, which can also be printed from the Web site at **www.sportsworkout.com/test.htm.** With the testing sheets, you will be able to use formulas to literally put your strength, power, endurance, and athletic ability to the test.

> You can find well-designed printable record-keeping charts at **www.sportsworkout.com/chart.htm** that are designed to work with any one of the provided routines, and testing sheets at **www.sportsworkout.com/test.htm** where you can test your progress in many fashions.

**When to increase:** Keeping records of your daily activity in the gym will allow you to determine when you are ready to increase the workload and by how much. Without well-kept records, your attempts to intensify your weight-training regimen will be made with hit or miss tactics. These tactics are not efficient ways to make gains because you will waste time by approximating your weight-loads and you may not be pushing yourself hard enough with the proper resistance. With well-kept records, you will know exactly when you need to increase the load and by how much.

**Where to start:** At one point or another, there will be instances when you will be unable to make it to the gym for extended periods of time. It may be because you become ill, experience a death in the family, or go on a vacation. The bottom line is there may be a time when you will stop your program and need to re-enter it. By keeping records, you will know exactly where you left off. Because you have taken time away from lifting, however, you will need to slightly decrease the load from where you left off, but you will have your records as a measuring stick. This is a very important aspect to training. If you take an extended period of time away from lifting without maintaining records, you will have to go by memory, which will result in trial and error once again.

**Observe your gains:** It is very important to be able to observe your gains for several reasons. The most important is that with well-kept records, you will be able to see which parts of the body you have made improvements in and which parts still need work. The records give you a sense of what changes need to be made for your next program to make up for these differences. You will want to saturate your next program with more exercises that train the weaker areas of your body, and this information can only be known with well-kept records.

**Motivation:** On top of monitoring your progress in the gym, record keeping provides you with the motivation to continue working harder and making bigger gains. You will literally be able to see on paper how you have progressed over time, which will inspire you to want to train harder. When people have hard evidence that they are actually making gains in the gym, it motivates them to continue making those gains.

**Overtraining:** How are record keeping and overtraining related? Even if you do not feel overtrained, you will be able to clearly see if you are overtrained by looking at your records. If, over time, you notice decreases from one day to the next in your records, the culprit may be overtraining. Overtraining may not always be the reason, but it very well could be. Other reasons could be changes in your eating or sleeping pattern or illness. In any case, record keeping will help you determine what the problem may be and how you can fix it.

Larger printable record keeping charts can be found at www.sportsworkout.com/chart.htm

**DATE:**    **BODY WT:**    Hours of Sleep:

**Time IN:**    **Time OUT:**    Other:

| EXERCISE: | | Set 1 | Set 2 | Set 3 | Set 4 | Set 5 |
|---|---|---|---|---|---|---|
| EXERCISE: | WEIGHT | | | | | |
| | DESIRED REPS | | | | | |
| | COMPLETED REPS | | | | | |
| EXERCISE: | WEIGHT | | | | | |
| | DESIRED REPS | | | | | |
| | COMPLETED REPS | | | | | |
| EXERCISE: | WEIGHT | | | | | |
| | DESIRED REPS | | | | | |
| | COMPLETED REPS | | | | | |
| EXERCISE: | WEIGHT | | | | | |
| | DESIRED REPS | | | | | |
| | COMPLETED REPS | | | | | |
| EXERCISE: | WEIGHT | | | | | |
| | DESIRED REPS | | | | | |
| | COMPLETED REPS | | | | | |
| EXERCISE: | WEIGHT | | | | | |
| | DESIRED REPS | | | | | |
| | COMPLETED REPS | | | | | |
| EXERCISE: | WEIGHT | | | | | |
| | DESIRED REPS | | | | | |
| | COMPLETED REPS | | | | | |
| EXERCISE: | WEIGHT | | | | | |
| | DESIRED REPS | | | | | |
| | COMPLETED REPS | | | | | |

**DATE:**    **BODY WT:**    Hours of Sleep:

**Time IN:**    **Time OUT:**    Other:

| EXERCISE: | | Set 1 | Set 2 | Set 3 | Set 4 | Set 5 |
|---|---|---|---|---|---|---|
| EXERCISE: | WEIGHT | | | | | |
| | DESIRED REPS | | | | | |
| | COMPLETED REPS | | | | | |
| EXERCISE: | WEIGHT | | | | | |
| | DESIRED REPS | | | | | |
| | COMPLETED REPS | | | | | |
| EXERCISE: | WEIGHT | | | | | |
| | DESIRED REPS | | | | | |
| | COMPLETED REPS | | | | | |
| EXERCISE: | WEIGHT | | | | | |
| | DESIRED REPS | | | | | |
| | COMPLETED REPS | | | | | |
| EXERCISE: | WEIGHT | | | | | |
| | DESIRED REPS | | | | | |
| | COMPLETED REPS | | | | | |
| EXERCISE: | WEIGHT | | | | | |
| | DESIRED REPS | | | | | |
| | COMPLETED REPS | | | | | |
| EXERCISE: | WEIGHT | | | | | |
| | DESIRED REPS | | | | | |
| | COMPLETED REPS | | | | | |
| EXERCISE: | WEIGHT | | | | | |
| | DESIRED REPS | | | | | |
| | COMPLETED REPS | | | | | |

**DATE:**    **BODY WT:**    Hours of Sleep:

**Time IN:**    **Time OUT:**    Other:

| EXERCISE: | | Set 1 | Set 2 | Set 3 | Set 4 | Set 5 |
|---|---|---|---|---|---|---|
| EXERCISE: | WEIGHT | | | | | |
| | DESIRED REPS | | | | | |
| | COMPLETED REPS | | | | | |
| EXERCISE: | WEIGHT | | | | | |
| | DESIRED REPS | | | | | |
| | COMPLETED REPS | | | | | |
| EXERCISE: | WEIGHT | | | | | |
| | DESIRED REPS | | | | | |
| | COMPLETED REPS | | | | | |
| EXERCISE: | WEIGHT | | | | | |
| | DESIRED REPS | | | | | |
| | COMPLETED REPS | | | | | |
| EXERCISE: | WEIGHT | | | | | |
| | DESIRED REPS | | | | | |
| | COMPLETED REPS | | | | | |
| EXERCISE: | WEIGHT | | | | | |
| | DESIRED REPS | | | | | |
| | COMPLETED REPS | | | | | |
| EXERCISE: | WEIGHT | | | | | |
| | DESIRED REPS | | | | | |
| | COMPLETED REPS | | | | | |
| EXERCISE: | WEIGHT | | | | | |
| | DESIRED REPS | | | | | |
| | COMPLETED REPS | | | | | |

**DATE:**    **BODY WT:**    Hours of Sleep:

**Time IN:**    **Time OUT:**    Other:

| EXERCISE: | | Set 1 | Set 2 | Set 3 | Set 4 | Set 5 |
|---|---|---|---|---|---|---|
| EXERCISE: | WEIGHT | | | | | |
| | DESIRED REPS | | | | | |
| | COMPLETED REPS | | | | | |
| EXERCISE: | WEIGHT | | | | | |
| | DESIRED REPS | | | | | |
| | COMPLETED REPS | | | | | |
| EXERCISE: | WEIGHT | | | | | |
| | DESIRED REPS | | | | | |
| | COMPLETED REPS | | | | | |
| EXERCISE: | WEIGHT | | | | | |
| | DESIRED REPS | | | | | |
| | COMPLETED REPS | | | | | |
| EXERCISE: | WEIGHT | | | | | |
| | DESIRED REPS | | | | | |
| | COMPLETED REPS | | | | | |
| EXERCISE: | WEIGHT | | | | | |
| | DESIRED REPS | | | | | |
| | COMPLETED REPS | | | | | |
| EXERCISE: | WEIGHT | | | | | |
| | DESIRED REPS | | | | | |
| | COMPLETED REPS | | | | | |
| EXERCISE: | WEIGHT | | | | | |
| | DESIRED REPS | | | | | |
| | COMPLETED REPS | | | | | |

# Test Yourself!

By testing yourself, you can visually see the gains you have made, and how extensive they have been. Provided for you at **www.sportsworkout.com/test.htm** are strength, power, endurance, and sport-specific tests so you can measure your progress in every fashion. You can also keep track of other important variables such as body weight, as well as muscle and waistline measurements.

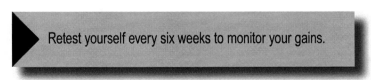

Retest yourself every six weeks to monitor your gains.

You can apply the strength, power, or endurance tests to any and all of the recommended exercises. However, it is suggested that you only test yourself in the bench press, leg press, military press, and lat pull because it would take days for you to test yourself in each of the recommended exercises. These four exercises are good indications of your overall fitness because they cover all of your major muscle groups. The bench press works your chest and triceps. The leg press covers your entire lower body. The lat pull has you working your lats and biceps. And military press trains your shoulders and traps.

The website provides you with several ways of testing yourself so that you will know exactly what you have improved in and what you may still need work on. For every non-weight-training related test, take the best of three tests to ensure the most accurate results.

# Conclusion

You are now ready to begin weight training for your sport. You have all of the information in front of you and expert-designed programs for your use, equipping you with the best methods available to improve your athletic potential. You also know how to apply the exercises properly. With hard work and determination, you will achieve any goals you set for yourself. Best of luck training and best of luck in your sport.

If you enjoyed this book and play other sports, or if you know someone who plays sports, be sure to check out other sport-specific training books and products at **www.sportsworkout.com**.

## Did you find the information in this book useful?

If you did, tell us about it and we'll send you a

# free gift!

All you have to do is tell us your:

*Name*

*Sport*

*Level of play (High School, College, Professional, Recreational)*

*Achievements (Championships, Tournaments won, Milestones)*

*A brief paragraph telling us how this book has helped your sport-specific performance*


Please send all replies to:
**athletes@sportsworkout.com**

# Do you play other sports?

The world's Largest Selection of Sport-Specific Weight Training Books

# Think About It

All Sports require strength in the **forearms, hands, and fingers.**

But do you exercise these muscles when you workout?
**Neither do most athletes.**

## Introducing the Sports Buddy!

The Sports Buddy was specifically designed for athletes that want to improve strength in their fingers, hands, and especially their forearms.

As just 12 inches in length, you can take the Sports Buddy anywhere.

It also has been specifically designed to fit both standard and Olympic style weights (see picture above).

**Not your average wrist roller. Not your average price.**
Just **$9.95** with this promo code: **010058** at

# Members Only

*sports*workout.com

## SportsWorkout.com

introduces Ryan Lee's Sport-Specific membership, the world's largest strength & conditioning online membership site!

**Even the best in the business agree this membership is invaluable:**

*"Simply the best and most complete sports training resource I've ever used. If you are serious about improving your sports performance, **I highly recommend joining today!**"*

**Duane Carlisle**
**NFL** Philadelphia Eagles Speed Consultant

*"I was just introduced to your site by a colleague of mine and I wanted to let you know how impressed I was. I will certainly recommend that my athletes check out your site."*

**Matt Nichol**
**NHL** Toronto Maple Leafs Head Strength Coach

## 12 months of access to:

➤ Over 5,000 pages of sport-specific articles, programs, and training tips created by professional strength coaches

➤ FREE UNLIMITED Sports Training Consulting via email with a detailed response guaranteed within 48 hours ($900 monthly value!)

➤ Members Only discussion forum with some of the brightest minds in sports training

➤ New articles, programs, video clips, & exercise images added every week

➤ Audio interviews with professional strength coaches

## Bonus Items!

➤ The Ultimate Guide to Weight Training for Sports ($37 value!)

➤ The Sports Buddy ($29.95 value!)

➤ Strength Ball ($8.95 value!)

➤ Fitness Training e-Charts ($15 value!)

## Free Shipping & Handling!

If you order now, we'll pay all shipping costs, and have all bonus items delivered to your door, absolutely free!

**For a very limited time, if you subscribe to our e-Training program all of this will be yours COMPLETELY FREE!**

**Just go to** `www.SportsWorkout.com/freemembership`

Even if you cancel your e-Training subscription, you still get to keep this 12 month Membership free of charge! There are no contracts to sign and you can cancel at any time for any reason, no questions asked.

Go to **www.SportsWorkout.com/freemembership** or call **1-866-S-WORKOUT (796-7568)** to Order!

# Think About It

All Sports require strength in the **forearms, hands, and fingers.**

But do you exercise these muscles when you workout?
**Neither do most athletes.**

## Introducing the Sports Buddy!

The Sports Buddy was specifically designed for athletes that want to improve strength in their fingers, hands, and especially their forearms.

As just 12 inches in length, you can take the Sports Buddy anywhere.

It also has been specifically designed to fit both standard and Olympic style weights (see picture above).

**Not your average wrist roller. Not your average price.**

Just **$9.95** with this promo code: **010058** at